Loving Work

For John,

Thanks for trusting me
with this great work
that I have been called
to. Blessings too, on
your work and on
CANISIUS !

Blessings,

Mike Hayes

Loving Work

A spiritual guide to
finding the work we love
and bringing love to the work we do

MIKE HAYES

ORBIS BOOKS

Maryknoll, New York 10545

Founded in 1970, Orbis Books endeavors to publish works that enlighten the mind, nourish the spirit, and challenge the conscience. The publishing arm of the Maryknoll Fathers and Brothers, Orbis seeks to explore the global dimensions of the Christian faith and mission, to invite dialogue with diverse cultures and religious traditions, and to serve the cause of reconciliation and peace. The books published reflect the views of their authors and do not represent the official position of the Maryknoll Society. To learn more about Maryknoll and Orbis Books, please visit our website at www.maryknollsociety.org.

Published by Orbis Books, Maryknoll, New York 10545–0302.

Manufactured in the United States of America.

Library of Congress Cataloging-in-Publication Data

Hayes, Mike, 1970–
    Loving work : a spiritual guide to finding the work we love and beginning to love the work we do / Mike Hayes.
        p. cm.
        ISBN 978–1–57075–988–8 (pbk.)
    1. Work—Religious aspects—Christianity. I. Title.
        BT738.5.H39 2012
        248.8'8—dc23
                                                                    2012022663

For Mom and Dad,
who guided me as best they could
and allowed me to discern who I needed to become. You are
in these pages and I love you for that.

To the Jesuits
who have served as my spiritual directors
throughout my life:
Fr. John Mullin, SJ; Fr. Jim McDermott, SJ;
Fr. Rocco Danzi, SJ; and Bro. Chris Derby, SJ.
You have all lived the Magis.

CONTENTS

PREFACE

Finally I am coming to the conclusion that my highest ambition is to be what I already am. That I will never fulfill my obligation to surpass myself unless I first accept myself, and if I accept myself fully in the right way, I will already have surpassed myself.

—THOMAS MERTON

I love having house guests and sharing my home with people from time to time. Occasionally, my wife and I will have long-term house guests—those who stay for a week or more. As the last few days of their stay arrives, I can feel myself growing anxious. I want to have my house back to myself. It's time for them to go home and for me to be able to relax fully.

In my own life, however, I've often treated God like a house guest, inviting him into some parts of my life but not others. At times, I have relegated religion to Sunday and service projects and haven't considered that God could possibly permeate the rest of my life. Perhaps I was even a house guest of God's who thought that I had overstayed my welcome and eschewed God from the other parts of life, assuming that God didn't care much about them.

My second big failure in life is that I often wore a mask. I pretended not to be hurt or vulnerable by wearing a "tough guy" mask. I often didn't tell the truth about myself on dates or in mixed company because I was afraid that others wouldn't like the "real me." I had to become someone different in order to be liked.

But Halloween is only once a year, and that's the only day where masks are positive. Further, God is not a house guest and, in fact, opens his home to us always, residing closer to our own hearts than we could possibly imagine.

This book is about *not* faking it. It's about living with intention, with honor, and with a sense of self-worth. It's about finding out who God has already made you to be and how you might go about becoming that person, how you can live the life you were born to live.

Studies show that mass attendance in the Catholic Church is at a low for recent times. Among millennial young adults perhaps only 10 percent or so attend mass on a weekly basis. There are some who argue that if we move that number to 20 percent, we will be doing great, that we will have a more faithful church with a smaller number like that.

I vehemently disagree. What we need as people of faith is an integration of faith in all matters of life. God is our lure and calls us into being more human, more alive than ever before.

This book is not based on a prosperity-based theology, meaning God wants you to be rich. Nor is this book based on what I call "trickle-down" spirituality, meaning if we educate and care for the elite members of our church, they will, in turn, instruct and inspire others.

No, this book is based on developing a spirituality of love. This love is based in passion not merely for what you do as a career, but also, and primarily, for who you are—who God has designed you to become with your own unique gifts and talents.

The title has two meanings. *Loving work* could refer to a passion one has for his or her career. I certainly love my work as a campus minister, spiritual director, and marriage minister in the Catholic Church. I firmly believe that we all can find work that we truly love, if we are willing to take some risks and perhaps even be a bit patient in developing that career.

But the larger question is whether the work we do is loving. Does our work express how much love we have for the world in which we live? Can we pinpoint how we make a contribution and how that contribution is based on a passion that only we alone may have?

That's work that's worth doing. And it will make you feel like you are not only on vacation every day. Rather, it will literally make you feel like yourself. And that's who God has called you to be anyway.

1

IS SOMETHING MISSING?

"What the hell is going on in here?"

It was a usual tantrum, hollered by any number of radio producers when things weren't going well. Today's tantrum was bellowed by Chris, one of my closest colleagues at WOR Radio in New York.

"The usual bullshit." I yelled back. "Schwartz is cranky, but I coddled him and he's as calm as a baby with his blanky now."

"Oh, brother," Chris sighed back. "And why do I come to work again?"

For the past four weeks or so Chris had been even crankier than our usual cranky show host. It was no coincidence that Chris celebrated his thirtieth birthday somewhere in the midst of those four weeks. So one day when we were both calm and things were running rather well, I dared to say to him, "So, turning thirty really sucks, huh?"

Chris's ears perked up, "Dude, how'd you know?"

I pressed even further. "Well, you've been cranky all month. Let me guess at what's wrong. You looked in the mirror on your thirtieth birthday and said, 'I'm thirty years old, and all I've done with my life is produce this silly radio show.'"

Chris smiled back at me and said: "Yeah! That's exactly right! How'd you know that?"

"Because I'm twenty-eight, and all I've ever done is *engineer* this silly radio show!"

It was the start of a year of deep discernment for both Chris and me. We both enjoyed being in radio, but something was missing, something different for each one of us. Chris was looking for something higher profile, a job with more responsibility and something more challenging. I just wanted to get out. My dream of being an on-air host was dwindling. Program directors liked me, but they wanted me to go and hone my craft in a smaller market. "You don't start an on-air career in New York, kid," was the mantra I heard often from the higher-ups.

The truth is that I had done remarkably well in radio for someone with no connections. I became a producer at the biggest all-sports station in the country, WFAN Radio in New York, and did some part-time reporting to boot. I got my voice on the air and covered a World Series and a bunch of other cool things, but time had run its course. I moved to all-talk WOR, where I did more of the same: lots of behind-the-scenes production and the occasional on-air opportunity. I covered the Yankee locker room for Bob Papa, now an accomplished sportscaster for NBC and HBO, and I did play-by-play and color analysis for a minor league baseball team in Yonkers, New York—my hometown. All of it was a great learning experience in so many ways.

But truth be told, I was bored. I didn't want to admit that to myself, but I was. I couldn't wait for games to be over some nights. I was tired of the inane claptrap of statistics and scores. All of it came to a head when

I received the opportunity to cover an NBA game one evening.

The game itself was rather uneventful. The Bulls, led by the incomparable Michael Jordan, were well on their way to a blowout victory over the hapless New Jersey Nets. In the third quarter Chris Morris, one of the Nets players, went up for a slam dunk and shattered the backboard.

"Idiot!" I thought. "Come on, let's roll the replacement backboard out and keep this bloodbath going."

But that was wishful thinking. For some reason the staff at the Meadowlands was unprepared for a broken backboard. It had to hammer in a new one, delaying the game for over a half hour. More than a quarter of the New Jersey faithful (or should I say, unfaithful?) headed for the exits. I phoned in a report to the station doing a one-on-one interview with Howie Rose, one of my favorite show hosts and a great mentor to me at The FAN. We talked simply about the incident and about how the crowd dispersed when it got impatient and didn't feel like sitting around.

Later on, when the game mercifully ended, we hit the locker room. I walked into the Bulls locker and ran smack dab into #23 himself, Michael Jordan.

"Whoa! Sorry, Michael!"

"It's cool!" he said. "Long night for all of us!"

Other reporters now had gathered around His Airness, and we began the customary post-game interview scrum.

The questions were customary ones. I can't even say I remember any of them, except one that I asked that was not related to the game. I asked him to comment on a story about Knicks player John Starks, who had been fined that day (I don't remember why).

"Got nothing to do with me."

"OK, thanks, Michael." A rather forgettable interview after a god-awful boring game.

I called the station and was asked what interviews I had recorded. I counted off:

"Chuck Daly, four cuts. Chris Morris, two cuts. Rick Mahorn, a preview cut for tomorrow. And four cuts of Jordan."

There was a long pause on the other end of the phone. Then the desk assistant said, "Michael Jordan?"

I replied, "Yeah, who else would it be?"

"Kid, Jordan doesn't usually talk much. Nice job."

"Thanks, I guess." I replied. "It's not all that big a deal."

"You should be much more excited about this than you are!" the voice at the other end of the phone screamed.

But I wasn't. I had just talked with perhaps the greatest NBA player of all time, and it didn't faze me in the least.

Now there's an element of professionalism here. Interviewing athletes was my job. In some ways it wasn't supposed to faze me to have someone of his stature in front of me. But let's face it. It was Michael Jordan. That's pretty cool for a young cub reporter's first NBA game.

I crashed at my college roommate's apartment that night. He asked how the game was, and I replied, "Horrible. Morris broke the backboard in a blowout, and it took them half an hour to fix it. I couldn't wait to get out of there. Oh, yeah, after the game I ran into Jordan and asked him a question."

He nearly choked on his dinner.

"You . . . talked . . . to . . . MICHAEL JORDAN?"

"Yeah, it's not that big a deal. Happens all the time. I talked to Reggie Jackson last week too!"

"Mike Hayes," he said, "you should be much more excited about this than you are!"

But I wasn't. There was something missing. What more did I want? More fame? A better job? More on-air opportunities? Or something else entirely? I couldn't put my finger on it at the time.

As you read through these chapters you'll find how I came to discern what it was that was missing and what I was really craving. And why I wouldn't trade my current calling for anything else.

This book is for those of you who think something is missing or don't like where your career is heading. Perhaps you've been at the same job and are just spinning your wheels? Perhaps you hate your job and want to make a change but you're too afraid to take the plunge? Maybe you're just out of college or graduate school and are feeling uneasy about your career choice or feel overwhelmed by the thought that perhaps you picked the wrong thing to study?

I've been there. And others have too. As you read on you'll hear a number of stories and suggestions from people who discerned similar questions and, more important, decided to do something about it. As a campus and young adult minister in the Catholic Church, I'd be a bit remiss if I didn't mention some of my favorite saints and even some colleagues and friends who've had a lot to say about discernment. Ignatius of Loyola, the founder of the Jesuits (a religious order of priests who primarily run universities and high schools), is one of my favorites, and you'll hear a lot about his story and how he came to change from being a dedicated soldier to becoming a great priest and eventually a saint. Saints are people who, simply put, become the best version of themselves. Some of them become officially recognized by the church, but others remain anonymous except to a certain few who knew of their lives and are assured that they are with God.

One of my favorite saints is Dave Connors. You probably have never heard of him. He was one of my college roommates. And he died at the young age of twenty-five after a long period of illness. Dave taught me a lot about living and even quite a bit about dying. You see, when we think about it, we're all dying every day—some of us just get there a bit faster than others. Dave knew that intuitively. In fact, Dave wondered often, in college, how much longer he might have to live. He spent some time being angry at God about being sick. He had a weak heart, diabetes, and a few other medical conditions. Still, Dave never wanted anyone to feel sad about him or have people let him cut corners because they felt sorry for him. "No, don't do it for me," was one of his oft-used phrases. He'd rather try and fail than not try at all.

Dave often appeared pale and sickly, and he was really underweight. I think he probably weighed approximately 120 pounds, and he stood about 5'7" or so. Often he'd walk up to a bouncer at a bar and pick a fight with him. It was ridiculous and would make us all laugh, the bouncer included. Dave realized he had a great gift for humor and he lived each and every day with laughter. I don't recall a single day when he didn't make someone laugh. He even won Fordham's standup comedy award—and it wasn't because people felt sorry for him. It was because he was laugh-out-loud funny. Even when a joke bombed—and he confessed that he sometimes told an awful joke on purpose so he could follow it up with a line like "Well, *that* went over like a fart in church"—the whole place would roar.

You see, Dave was really just being himself—the best version of himself. He only lived twenty-five years, but he was truly alive. He stays alive each time I recall that he knew how to live and that he didn't waste a single day. He even made the hospital chaplain, a young seminarian and a fairly serious fellow, laugh until his sides hurt.

I have come to believe that discovering who you are and living your life in a way that best expresses who you are is actually what God asks of us. More important, I believe that it is how God designed us and that our purpose in this life is to discover all we can about ourselves at our deepest level, so that we can become all that God believes that we can become. In doing so, we discover much about ourselves, but we also discover much about God. We'll spend much of our first few chapters discussing this.

Our work can and in many ways *should* reflect this design as well. After all, God doesn't want us to spend a great majority of our time doing something that we're not really called to do. Sometimes our job will be directly related to our "calling," and sometimes it is just a way to make money so we can spend our recreational time on our calling. We'll spend another chapter discussing this in depth.

Where are we called to be? How do we find meaningful work? Who might help us along the way? There have been a lot of people who have helped me in my various walks of life. Moreover, the question of place is one that can and often does fluctuate throughout life as we feel God's call pulling us to different places and in different ways. If you're considering a career change, or if you love your work but hate the company or dislike your coworkers, or even just feel like something is missing even though work is ultimately satisfying . . . you'll want to pay particular attention to Chapter 5.

Lastly, Jesus of Nazareth, gives us a model to follow when he meets the rich young man in the gospel:

Just then a man came up to Jesus and asked, "Teacher, what good thing must I do to get eternal life?"

"Why do you ask me about what is good?" Jesus replied. "There is only One who is good. If you want enternal life, keep the commandments."

"Which ones?" he inquired.

Jesus replied, "You shall not murder, you shall not commit adultery, you shall not steal, you shall not give false testimony, honor your father and mother,and love your neighbor as yourself."

"All these I have kept," the young man said. "What do I still lack?"

Jesus answered, "If you want to be perfect, go, sell your possessions and give to the poor, and you will have treasure in heaven. Then come, follow me."

When the young man heard this, he went away sad, because he had great wealth.

Then Jesus said to his disciples, "Truly I tell you, it is hard for someone who is rich to enter the kingdom of heaven. Again I tell you, it is easier for a camel to go through the eye of a needle than for someone who is rich to enter the kingdom of God."

When the disciples heard this, they were greatly astonished and asked, "Who then can be saved?"

Jesus looked at them and said, "With man this is impossible, but with God all things are possible." (Matt 19:16–26)

Jesus sees the rich young man for who he can become. He's already a pretty good man, but does he want to settle for the comfort that he's become accustomed to? Or does he want a lot more? Giving up his riches might have allowed him to be free from some burden, or perhaps his wealth kept him a safe distance from where God was really inviting him to look more deeply at how he was living. Life is more than simply following the rules. There's also what those rules call us to become as well. He followed the rules, but he didn't really embrace them.

The poor in Jesus' society were outcasts, people who others believed were poor because they were cursed by God. In the Gospels Jesus refutes this notion that was ingrained in his society. So when he asks the rich man to become poor, it's just too much for him to handle. He can't see that embedded in the commandments of not murdering or committing adultery or coveting is the law that needs to be written on the heart, namely, to not do these things because all people have human dignity; we are called to serve everyone and restore dignity to those who are deprived of it.

The rich young man simply missed his calling, and the disciples aren't far behind him. "Who then, can be saved?" they ask. Why? Because being rich was thought to be an outward sign of God's favor. So if the rich man can't get into heaven, well, who can? Those who give up everything to become all that God calls them to be.

Now, in today's times, that doesn't necessarily mean that we have to become homeless in order to find where God calls us—although some have found that living a lot more simply frees them to concentrate on their lives. But often something gets in our way. Something prohibits us from believing that we can be *that* good. Something gets in our way of becoming all that we can be.

What might that be for you? Cardinal Francis George at a World Youth Day event said during a private audience with a group of American young people: "We're all in this great big Catholic club. We've traveled thousands of miles to be in Sydney to see the pope and show the world that we're united in faith. But in each and every one of our hearts, there's something that keeps us from fully committing our lives to Jesus."

God is calling us. In the next few chapters I ask you to consider the person you are becoming. What kind of person would you like to become? What gives you a passionate desire for life? What is your image of God? What might God be calling you to become?

The journey to yourself and to God awaits.

Questions for Discussion/Reflection:

- How can you be the best version of yourself?
- What might you think about doing in order to get more in touch with being the best version of yourself?
- What keeps you from fully committing yourself to becoming the person God is calling you to be?

2

WHO AM I?

The phone rang as it did many times that day in the newsroom, and I picked it up as one of my usual desk assistant duties.

"FAN Sports, Mike Hayes," my usual greeting.

"Mike, it's Joel. I need to talk to Gelb."

Joel didn't sound right. Joel Hollander was the boss, the station's general manager. It sounded as if he was upset. My first thought was that something had happened on the air that annoyed him, and he wanted to talk to Bob Gelb, the producer of the famed afternoon show, "Mike and the Mad Dog."

"I'm not sure where he is right now, Joel. Something I can help you with?"

"Mike, something bad has happened. My little daughter died today. Can you try to find Bob, please? I need to let the guys know."

The station was devastated. Carly Jenna was Joel's youngest, and she died of Sudden Infant Death Syndrome (SIDS), also known as crib death. It was right around Easter. My only thought was that it had to be the worst thing to ever happen to anyone. Joel would need to bury his child. She was only four months old. I had to work the day of the funeral at the station. I figured Joel would understand and would probably be happy that someone was taking care of things, but my colleagues and I were visibly shaken by Carly's death.

My cousin, Mary Lou, had lost her baby, Jaime, to SIDS not long before. Babies are not supposed to die.

I didn't know Joel well. He was the general manager, the head honcho of the biggest all-sports radio station in the country.

In other words, he was a big deal. The fact that he even knew my name was an important connection.

He was nice to me when we'd see each other, but he interacted more with the suits upstairs in sales than he did with us in programming. But even though I didn't know him well, the next few days were tough. I remember being glad that Joel was religious. And the thought Joel and his wife, Susan, would rely on their Jewish faith over the next many months comforted me. They went on to inspire me, taking one step further than anyone would need to in deciding to heal from this awful death. Joel and Susan founded the CJ Foundation for SIDS, named after their daughter, Carly Jenna, and they would raise countless dollars for research and counseling for parents who lost a child to SIDS.

Some months later we held the first WFAN radiothon for Joel's foundation. I found myself volunteering some extra time. I just felt I needed to do something for Joel's family. I headed down to the World Financial Center and asked my colleagues what I could do to help. I assisted the line producer with the broadcast for a good deal of the afternoon. And then I headed back to the station to produce the evening shows.

Usually I would simply head home, but something kept gnawing at me.

"If that was your kid, you'd be there all night." I thought.

So I went back to the World Financial Center. Perhaps they'd need help on the overnight.

They did. We actually had a lot of fun. I was "the kid." I was twenty-four. One of the sales assistants teased me about being so young. Her husband had held a job longer than I had been alive. That got a great laugh from all of us, me included. We spent that whole night counting pledge bills, taking phone pledges, tallying numbers, and relaying information back to the station. We'd put parents on the air to talk with our usual macho sports talk hosts about what they went through. It was a long night and the topic of conversation was dreadful. We had to continue to inspire others without deeply depressing them. A tough balance to be sure.

As the sun began to rise over Manhattan, volunteers made their way to our call center. Tired though I was, I began to coordinate them into teams and give them the crash course in taking phone pledges.

"Credit cards are great!" I told the crowd. "That means we get paid first. So if they can use plastic, let them."

My direct supervisor and our executive producer, Eric Spitz, came to me and said, "When did you get here?"

"I've been here." I replied.

"All night?"

"Yeah, not a big deal. I don't have to work until tomorrow. So I figured I'd pitch in."

"That's a lot more than pitching in," he said.

I blew him off. "No biggie, Eric. Just doing what I can. It's a tough day and I'm able to be here. So whatever."

As we tallied the final numbers, I sat back and was pretty proud of the work that had been done that day. I heard the promotions director say, "Wow, Mike Hayes really went the extra mile. He was just so great."

I wasn't buying it. I was just doing what I'd want someone to do for me, if I were going through something like that. I'd tell myself that it was nothing more and nothing less.

Now at this time, I'd like to point out that I was an OK radio producer/reporter. I did a good job, but I wasn't exactly setting the world on fire. I was starting at the bottom in a pretty high-profile industry. More often than not, I spent my days being bored, hoping that this job would lead to something more exciting, hopefully on-air as a sportscaster.

But had I really been paying attention, I would have noticed how much I came alive when I was working on that radiothon. Years later I would find myself plugging away behind the soundboard for six straight hours during another radiothon at WOR for Variety, a children's charity run by several local celebrities.

Even when I was doing some of the fun jobs I was given, I'd be more interested in the more human-interest stories that served as filler on slow sports days. When David Cone won the Cy Young Award, I mentioned to Steve Somers, one of our overnight hosts, that I was happy about it because he was the spokesperson for the Rheumatoid Arthritis Foundation. My mother suffers from that disease, and I know how crushing it can be. It turned out that Somers's mother had died of complications from the disease.

"That disease is a killer, and nobody knows about it!"

I replied, "Let's bring it up on the air!"

So we did. Someone called in complaining that David Cone won the Cy Young Award instead of Jimmy Key.

Caller: "Steve, aren't you upset about this?"

Steve: "No."

Caller: "Why not?"

Steve: "Well, Key may well deserve the award, but I'm very happy for David Cone because he's the spokesperson for the Rheumatoid Arthritis Foundation."

Steve launched into a touching monologue about how his mother had suffered and how my mom is dealing with the disease. If winning the award is good for that foundation, then he couldn't help but be happy.

It was a human moment, filled with honesty and emotion. How Somers kept his composure I'll never know. I know my eyes were filled with tears for most of the overnight. The next day the sports media critic at the *New York Daily News*, Bob Raissman, wrote a full-page story about Somers's candor. Steve called me at the office from home the next day.

"Did you see the paper? *Raissman!*"

I replied that I had and offered him congratulations.

His humble response was classic, "Here we are trying to fill time on the overnight, and we get points for getting all sentimental and humanitarian already!"

I laughed and told him that the show meant a lot to both of us, whether it was in the paper the next day or not. While I'm glad it was, it certainly wasn't our motivation.

There's a great word: *motivation*. What motivates you? What brings you to a place where you'd be doing what it is you are doing freely, perhaps without the need for reward?

For myself, the thought of being thanked for working on the radiothon never entered the picture. I was really happy working that night, and more important, I was proud of the work that I was doing.

Joel Hollander showed up in the control room the day after the radiothon and told me how much he and his family appreciated all the work I had done. I can still see myself shrugging my shoulders.

"Aw, gee, Joel. It was the least I could do. You're welcome. Anytime." We shook hands and an overwhelming feeling of joy came over me as Joel left the studio.

You'd think I would have awakened then and asked Joel for a job with the foundation. But no. I was in broadcasting. I could almost hear myself convincing me that doing good work was fine and that anyone would feel this way after doing a good deed for another.

But the truth is that I was not born to be another Marv Albert. I was born to be Mike Hayes. And, in fact, I can't be anyone else, try though I did. While being in the media made many of my colleagues express themselves in a wonderful way, and from time to time

I showed some real promise, it wasn't ultimately the best expression of who I am.

Thomas Merton always wondered if he was becoming the best person he could be. He discovered that becoming a saint means simply to be who you are. To be all that you can be, nothing more, but more important, nothing less. Saints are ordinary people who become all that they are called to be. And if that's the case, well, then we should all hope to be saints. It's in our best interest to be saints. But most of the time we quiet that urge down. We become humble and shrink from the holiness that is within us.

And that is simply bad theology. We often get too tied up with how bad and sinful we are. Catholics and Jews especially have this cloud of guilt hanging over them. Arthur Schwartz, a wonderful radio food critic that I worked with at WOR, once chided me because he had told me that I had done a great job producing the show one day and I attempted to talk him out of it. "Eh," I shrugged, "It could have been a whole lot better if I hadn't put that one caller through." Now there's always room for being critical, but I think I was taking it to a new extreme. "Michael," Arthur said to me, "You're Catholic and I'm Jewish, and we have enough guilt here to sink a fleet of ships between us. We don't need any more."

We both laughed, but then I realized that he was right. I was a bit afraid to claim success. I was a kid who came from the streets of Yonkers, the son of a custodian, who somehow managed to get to Fordham and graduate. Then I somehow ended up being able to work at two of the biggest radio stations in the country. Not too shabby. I'm pretty proud of that, looking back. I saw a dream and I went for it, and it was pretty close to what I imagined.

The truth is that sometimes we're too afraid to be saints—to be all that we can be. We think that we don't deserve the title of saint, that we're not good enough or strong enough or there are too many people out there who deserve to be called saints much more than we do.

Dorothy Day, the great founder of the Catholic Worker movement, used to shy away from the saint title. "Now don't you call me a saint!" she'd say. "I won't be dismissed that easily."

Whenever I hear that quotation, I always think, "Well, she must have been a joy to live in community with!"

But Dorothy Day really meant that in a most positive way. Most of us would say without hesitation the words "I'm no saint." We know our own flaws. We can be hard on ourselves, but even worse than that, we sometimes don't think we can become what God knows we can be. We don't believe that our hearts can stretch a bit farther than we think they can.

Each time I read the Gospels, I'm convinced that this unworthiness of the sainthood title is nothing new. Simon Peter can be any one of us who says all too quickly that he or she is not a saint.

Then he made the disciples get into the boat and precede him to the other side, while he dismissed the crowds.

After doing so, he went up on the mountain by himself to pray. When it was evening he was there alone.

Meanwhile the boat, already a few miles offshore, was being tossed about by the waves, for the wind was against it.

During the fourth watch of the night, he came toward them, walking on the sea.

When the disciples saw him walking on the sea they were terrified. "It is a ghost," they said, and they cried out in fear.

At once [Jesus] spoke to them, "Take courage, it is I; do not be afraid."

Peter said to him in reply, "Lord, if it is you, command me to come to you on the water."

He said, "Come." Peter got out of the boat and began to walk on the water toward Jesus.

But when he saw how [strong] the wind was he became frightened; and, beginning to sink, he cried out, "Lord, save me!"

Immediately Jesus stretched out his hand and caught him, and said to him, "O you of little faith, why did you doubt?"

After they got into the boat, the wind died down.

Those who were in the boat did him homage, saying, "Truly, you are the Son of God." (Matt 14:22–33)

We are all a bit like Peter. We do great things, and then we doubt ourselves, holding on to fear. Might we be afraid that we might be even greater than we think we are? Peter could walk on water, but once the winds blew, he didn't believe he could withstand them. Essentially, he psyched himself out.

Ben Zander, the leader of the Boston Philharmonic, has a great video on ted.com. If you ever need to be inspired, I highly recommend it. He talks about his passion for classical music:

> "I'm not going to go on until every single person in this room, downstairs and in Aspen, and everybody else looking, will come to love and understand classical music. So that's what we're going to do.
>
> "Now, you notice that there is not the slightest doubt in my mind that this is going to work if you look at my face, right? It's one of the characteristics of a leader that he not doubt for one moment the capacity of the people he's leading to realize whatever he's dreaming. Imagine if Martin Luther King had said, I have a dream. Of course, I'm not sure they'll be up to it" *(laughter)*.

We are called to be people of passion. Imagine how you'd be if you woke up an realized that you were going to be doing something that you are truly passionate about. How would you express yourself? How would you act? Wouldn't that be exciting?

Sometimes that passion can be best expressed in the workplace, and sometimes it's best expressed outside your career. Sometimes your passion is directly linked up with your job, as my job in ministry is. Living out who you are may best be expressed at home with your family, or with friends, or in your community. Regardless, that expression is your true self—it is how you express the person you're called to be. You might be able to make that into the way you make your living, but that's not the point. You *need* to be this person, paid or volunteer. And even when you fight against it, it creeps up on you, haunting you, calling your name, waking you up in the middle of the night.

A great example from my own life. I wasn't exactly unhappy when I was working in radio producing and reporting. It was a fun job with some great colleagues and many are still great friends today. I covered sports and worked on advice talk shows and, in general, lived day to day pretty well. The issue at hand was that while this was pretty great, it wasn't a passion. I could really take or leave it most of the time. I get up most days now breaking down the door to get to my job, as opposed to waking up and wondering what's going to be in store for me. I go to work assuming that the day is going to be great.

Now that sounds rather rosy. Bad things still happen, colleagues still frustrate me, and I get annoyed by all kinds of injustices and frankly, meanness that exists even within the church. But by and large, I feel that there's so much more that I can contribute. I feel connected to mission and have a sense of purpose. I look forward to students and young adults who are challenging to me in spiritual direction. I can't wait for the next retreat (you should see me already planning the next one as a retreat comes to an end!). I hate taking a day off because it's one more day that I don't get to live that passion.

But imagine if we could really live that kind of enthusiasm often? Some days we just don't have it in us, granted. But when we have more days when we just don't have the energy to get up and go to work fully charged up with positive energy and hope to make a difference, even in some small way, perhaps that should say something to us.

The solution to this is not to merely up and quit one's current job. *(Legal note: Mike Hayes never ever told you anywhere in this book to quit your job. That decision rests with you alone.)* The solution is to ask what might give you the energy you need to make it through the week, to express that passion that haunts you.

Do we make excuses? "Oh, I'll do that next year!" Or "I don't have time for that!" Or "If I do this I might lose some money."

A colleague tells of meeting a salesman who got promoted one year to sales manager—and suddenly became miserable. When asked about it, he pointed out how little sales he was really doing. Instead he was keeping track of other people's sales abilities and trying to push them to sell more and more. He wasn't particularly good at this, and people began to resent him.

"I was so much happier when I was a sales guy."

My colleague asked him to tell him about what he liked most about being a sales guy. And suddenly he became vibrant and alive—filled with enthusiasm. He talked about the way he'd prepare his sales pitch and how he liked finding new clients and talking with people all day long, how he liked getting out of the office to go have lunch with new potential customers, how much enthusiasm he had for selling the product he represented, and how he thought people really loved the product once they knew about it. He practically sold my colleague on the product right there.

"Tom," my colleague pondered, "Would you get fired if you asked your boss if you could go back to being a salesman? Would people look down on you or would you feel horrible about yourself—like you had failed?"

"No, that wouldn't happen. They'd just let me return to my old job. Maybe some folks would think I failed, but seriously, I think it would be a relief. If only I could do it!"

"Why can't you?" my colleague pondered.

"I can't! I'd lose twenty thousand dollars a year if I did!"

"Tom, were you making a good living before the promotion?"

"Yes, I did fine."

"Well, then, congratulations, Tom. You've just named the price of your happiness and it's twenty thousand dollars. That's great! Most people never can name this but you've nailed it down to the penny! My price is much higher—but more power to you if yours is only twenty thousand."

Tom really thought about this, and eventually he made some changes. But many others don't.

What's the price of your happiness? Are you avoiding living a bit of your passion in favor of a few extra bucks? Could you live your passion and still make a decent living?

What is it that is haunting you? You might not need to make drastic changes in your life in order to live with more passion. It might be as simple as filling out an application or volunteering a bit of time—or even spending a bit of time in prayer with God asking for some guidance and asking yourself some important questions.

If you do, you may be on the way to becoming a saint, the best version of who God calls you to be. Nothing more, but, more important, nothing less.

Questions for Discussion/Reflection

- Have you ever thought that you could become a saint? Why or why not?
- Are you afraid of success? What might be holding you back from trying something new or exploring new possibilities?
- What's the price of your happiness? What would you have to give up in order to live your passion?

3

IF YOU COULD BE ANYTHING

"So, what's her name?"

I had been working for about an hour, at top speed, and had loads of enthusiasm that day. And so, Arthur Schwartz, the host of "Food Talk," the show I was producing at the time for WOR Radio, assumed I had met an attractive woman somewhere.

My reply was, "I'm not sure what you mean."

Arthur said, "Look, I haven't seen you this excited in months. Who is she? Is she really cute? And where did you meet her this weekend? I want the story . . . *now*."

"Well, truthfully," I blushed, "I was on a Catholic retreat this weekend, so I guess the woman's name is Mary, and I met her walking the stations of the cross."

Arthur laughed a hearty belly laugh. "And here I was thinking the altar boy hooked up! So what was so good about this retreat that has made you all excited?"

I said, "Well they're just awesome! I've been leading retreats for my parish and learned to lead them from the Jesuits at Fordham. I love bringing people together and having them inspire one another with their stories. We end up finding that we all have the same fears and hopes for our lives, that we want meaningful lives."

"Hmmmf," Arthur mumbled. "Sounds like you really enjoyed it. Let's get to work. We have a show to produce."

Later in the day Arthur and I were again alone. He took me aside and said, "So, why are you working here?"

I replied, "Um, I ask myself that question three times a week, but I guess I'm hoping that one day I'll get some opportunity to do something on the air somewhere."

Arthur said, "Is that your dream?"

I replied, "Well, I guess so. It's all I've thought about since college."

Arthur got a very serious look on his face and said, "Let me tell you something. You're not happy here. I love you, and you do fine work, but I think you're called to do so much more with your life than produce my radio show, or anyone else's. I even think you're called to do more than be on the air."

I got upset. "Look, if you're trying to get rid of me . . . "

Arthur said, "Well I am kind of trying to get rid of you—but in a good way. Look, your work is fine. But wouldn't you rather be spending your time doing something you truly love?"

The wheels in my head were spinning.

Arthur continued, "Let me tell you something. I worked at the *Daily News* forever. And I hated that office building. It was just not an atmosphere I liked being in. But I loved expressing my opinion about food, and I was good at it. So I was at a crossroads. I went to a counselor and asked her for help in seeing the big picture. She asked me one question: 'If you could be anything, what would you be doing tomorrow?'"

"Interesting exercise!" I retorted.

"Indeed," said Arthur. "I started to take the high road and said, 'Well maybe I'd be a lawyer and do lots of pro bono work . . . or a doct—' but the counselor cut me off and told me not to answer with a job but to answer with a way of being in the world."

"A way of being?" I inquired. "What's that mean?"

"Well, she asked me how I would spend my time if I didn't have to pay my mortgage or hold down a job. If I just had to exist. What would be my favorite thing to do?"

"Well, it sure as hell wasn't being at the paper," I said.

"Correct!" And Arthur told me that he answered her immediately. "I told her I'd sit at home in my underwear and laugh at my own jokes."

Now that I had that image . . . And just before lunch too.

But Arthur quickly rebounded. "Guess what?" he said to me.

"I don't know, what?"

"I'm a writer. I can do this!"

I laughed, and we began to talk about how Arthur likes being more introverted and how he doesn't mind some extroverted behavior, as long as he's talking about what he loves. So by the end of his counseling he took a huge risk and quit his job as food editor and kept a one-hour radio show, along with deciding to write more books. Leaving the editor job enabled him to propose more books and to write more often, test more recipes, and do more marketing events for the books.

He ended up happier and with more book sales than ever.

It was quite a tale. Then he turned to me and asked, "So, what about you?"

"What about me?" I said.

Arthur rolled his eyes, "What would you do if you could do anything tomorrow?"

I stammered and said that I had no idea.

"Well, think about it and let me know," Arthur said wisely.

For the next three nights I found it hard to sleep. I had dreams (nightmares really) of not knowing what would bring me true satisfaction. Arthur had awakened the sleeping giant.

I went back to him and yelled, "You know, I hate you and your stupid question! I haven't slept soundly since we talked."

"Not my fault," Arthur said. "You're the one who needs to work out the issues you have."

"Dude, you can't do this to me. What help can you give me?"

Arthur smiled and said, "Look, think of a time when you felt really excited in life. I'll even help you pick one out. How about those retreats you run?"

"Sure," I said. "That's an excellent example. It's my favorite thing to do."

Arthur said, "Well why don't you do *that* for a living?"

"Are you kidding me? I'd starve!"

Arthur quickly challenged me. "You don't know that. All you know is you're scared that you won't make enough money to earn a living. But you might. Call my friend in Litchfield, Connecticut, who runs the retreat house there. Talk to her. It seems as though she does all right. Call your priest friend who taught you how to lead these retreats and see what he tells you. I'm not letting you stop with that lame excuse. *Do the research.*"

I promised to do it but wasn't quite sure why. There was no way I was called to do this. Arthur saw my skepticism.

"All right, look, close your eyes. Now, you're waking up tomorrow. You have no obligations, you have no bills to pay or responsibilities. Just exist for one day. What would you do?"

"*I don't know,*" I shouted.

Arthur said calmly, Well, look, you mentioned that you loved sharing stories with people on retreat. Might you do that? You even said it was your favorite thing to do. I'm going to make a giant leap and say that you'd probably do something like that."

I weakly concurred.

"Now tell me why you like doing retreats," Arthur asked.

"Well . . . people hear the stories of others and how they've drawn out meaning from the things that have happened to them. The stories are real stories, not some kind of pie-in-the-sky hodgepodge of religion. The strength of the retreats is that they are real stories from real people. People like that, and they are inspired by it."

Arthur, a great listener, said, "But what do *you* like about this? You told me what the retreat attendees like."

"Hey!" I said, "You're right! I like the fact that they are inspired by what we do, that I am the conduit for their meaning-making." My voice went up three octaves. I was smiling, and I literally jumped up out of my seat.

Arthur said, "Now we're getting somewhere. So if you could inspire others every day in some way, would that make you want to leap out of bed in the morning?"

"Hell, yeah!" I shouted.

"Well, go do that," Arthur said. "And get the hell outta here!"

Being One with the Spirit

The spiritually connected life is about noticing things. Where are you most happy? Who are you with, and what are you doing when you feel most alive? Who and what bring you lasting joy? Arthur believed that I needed to look at my life a lot more deeply than I had been doing.

St. Ignatius of Loyola thought the same of his followers. He asked them to notice the highlights of their day in an examen (a daily review of the events of your day). Noticing where your joys and deep sorrows are helps with discovering what your true gift to the world might be. Ignatius uses the word *consolation* to describe those moments when we feel "in tune" with ourselves and *desolation* for the times when everything is out of whack. In hindsight, I find it interesting that Arthur, a semi-practicing Jew, had been teaching me discernment tools that the Catholic Church had taught for hundreds of years.

He led me to dispel the fears I had about retreat masters not making enough money. It turns out they do just fine, probably better than I was doing in radio then. He also led me to examine why I was still in radio to begin with.

I had worked at two of the biggest stations in the country doing mostly behind the scenes work and some street and locker-room reporting. I was pretty good on the air when I got an opportunity. I did a year of minor league baseball play by play to add to my college radio play-by-play experience. I wanted to be the next Vin Scully, the legendary voice of the Dodgers.

So I decided to interview all of the people I knew who had the job I wanted. At that time Bob Papa was the radio voice of New York Giants football. Mike Breen was the voice of the Knicks. And Gary Cohen was the radio voice of the New York Mets. I cornered all of them at some point and asked them why they loved doing what they did and what they hated about their jobs as well. There were some common themes; for example, they loved watching sports for a living and having a high-paying, high-profile job. But they disliked being away from family, the pressure, and the tense environment.

Their dislikes were things I didn't like about my job as a producer. I never saw friends or family; I was too busy working all the time. I always felt under pressure. Sometimes I thrived on that, but other times I was very uncomfortable. The loves were obvious to me. But after a year of doing minor league ball the novelty had worn off. I wasn't getting a huge thrill from being on the air. I'm sure that others never get tired of it. Chris "Mad Dog" Russo can never wait to get into that chair and start his radio show.

But that wasn't me.

So while the loves were unquestionably attractive to me, they weren't motivating me. I can remember what I said to someone later in the day.

"Do you know what would make me motivated to be a sportscaster? Doing it for the blind, so they'd get some enjoyment out of a descriptive broadcast. Marty Glickman (the famed dean of broadcasters) used to say that there was a blind man who loved listening to him and would write to him and tell him how he had been his eyes for years. I think that's why I really fell in love with broadcasting. I wanted to help someone see. Marty was using that as a way to remind us to be descriptive, and I got caught up in the altruism of that."

My friend Paul remarked, "You know Mike, that's the part you took seriously in college. If your broadcast wasn't descriptive enough, you'd get all pissed off. Someone told you once that your play by play wasn't entertaining, and you said that it wasn't supposed to entertain, it was supposed to describe the action."

I remembered that. And it got me off the fence. I began to think that perhaps I had chosen wrongly. Perhaps I had wasted nearly ten years of my life, when I could have been doing something else, something I found more exciting, even fulfilling.

I wanted to be inspiring.

So I went home and wrote down a hundred ways to be inspiring. Some I could do at home, or with friends, or with coworkers. While I was determined to get a new career, I still had to make a living until I found the right thing to jump to. So I decided that I would bring my new attitude to work. That year's radiothon was one of the most memorable ones for me. I volunteered my entire day at WOR to working it, and I even donated the day's pay to the charity. I called my old colleagues at WFAN and asked them if it would be all right if I came and donated some time to their radiothon. I spent more time in my parish and even asked a friend to come in fifteen minutes early on our Sunday shift so I could get to 5:15 mass on time. I hadn't made a move yet. But I was excited to be living differently.

The next move was to learn how to do Ignatius's examen. The examen is a type of daily prayer. It was the prayer that Ignatius required the Jesuits to do twice daily if they didn't have time to pray more often because the demands of the world were so great. The steps to the examen are simple, and the prayer itself should take about ten minutes, sometimes a bit longer if the day has been particularly rich.

The Examen

1. *Find a quiet place where you are comfortable.*

The place can be indoors or outdoors but you should be able to concentrate and not be concerned about any other matters. Walking works for some, but Ignatius discouraged that. I find it helpful on some days and not so helpful on others. Some of my students find the car a good place to do the examen, but I often chide them not to do it when the car is in motion, but instead do it in the parking lot or garage.

2. *Think of one moment of gratitude from the past day.*

This should be whatever comes to mind instantly. My dog's warmth on my lap, my wife's kiss hello, even a tasty salad have been some things that I've found as my simple opportunity to give thanks, knowing that all gifts come from God.

3. *Pray to the Holy Spirit for clear vision.*

We all come with our own biases and judgments. As we look to the events of our lives we need to see those with new eyes—to see what is actually happening and not what we believe is happening. For example, I had a huge fight with my sister once. When I reviewed the fight again in my mind, I could see clearly not only where she was being hurtful, but where I was being hurtful as well. I could even see how I led her to defend herself against my hurtful remarks bringing the fight into a full-force shouting match. I even saw the evil pleasure I took in getting a rise out of her. It was enough to see clearly. I reached for the phone and called to apologize (which was my moment of gratitude the next day, by the way). So we consider our moments, not as we experienced them the first time, but rather, how God experienced watching us.

4. *Review your day.*

Consider all the moments of the day from waking until the present. Some moments you'll naturally linger on more than the others. Those are the moments that God is calling you to look at more deeply with those new eyes. Just notice what happens in those moments and especially notice your feelings. Don't judge any of it. Just notice. *Today I was playing with my niece and I really looked happy when I was doing that.* Or, *Today I had to work with that woman that everyone hates in the office. I looked like I was going to the electric chair as I walked into her office.*

Ask yourself where you felt most consoled during the day? Where did you feel most desolate? Just notice those moments for what they are. Sometimes a pattern will develop. *Every time I am with Jim, I feel like we can conquer the world.* Or, *Every time I eat lunch with the accountants in my office, I become a horrible gossip.*

5. Have a heart-to-heart talk with Jesus.

This is an opportunity to tell Jesus anything you want in prayer about the past day. Perhaps you share some great insight or offer joyful words of thanksgiving. Perhaps you ask for forgiveness. Perhaps you ask for strength because you are frustrated or in need of guidance. Whatever the case, use the time wisely and speak from the heart.

6. End your time with an Our Father.

Doing the examen each day helps you see where you are most called. For me, retreats or doing one-on-one direction with students are usually the two places that I find myself in a most joyous place. Arguing with someone or having to defend myself from another's attack often brings desolation to me. When I was in radio my most consoling moments were never in the studio, at a game, or even while broadcasting. They almost always were when I was with people, talking about things that mattered more than a simple radio show.

Doing the examen also helped center me on Arthur's big question: "If you could be anything . . . " a lot easier each day. Our desires sometimes change over time, and doing the examen can help us notice where we feel different about some previous decisions.

Sometimes a person might help us discern. A spiritual director or even a secular counselor (vocational counseling is one of the many fields here) might be someone who can assist us in thinking more critically about our path.

But the main idea is to pray, to take some time away each day and to pray. One also should take time away for retreat, an extended period of time where we are "off the clock" and away from our usual mode.

Jesus can be a great example for us as we consider prayer as a part of our lives.

> Then Jesus was led by the Spirit into the desert to be tempted by the devil.
>
> He fasted for forty days and forty nights, and afterward he was hungry.
>
> The tempter approached and said to him, "If you are the Son of God, command that these stones become loaves of bread."
>
> He said in reply,
>
> "It is written:
>
> 'One does not live by bread alone, but by every word that comes forth from the mouth of God.'"
>
> Then the devil took him to the holy city, and made him stand on the parapet of the temple, and

said to him, "If you are the Son of God, throw yourself down. For it is written:

'He will command his angels concerning you'
and 'with their hands they will support you,
lest you dash your foot against a stone.'"

Jesus answered him, "Again it is written, 'You shall not put the Lord, your God, to the test.'"

Then the devil took him up to a very high mountain, and showed him all the kingdoms of the world in their magnificence, and he said to him, "All these I shall give to you, if you will prostrate yourself and worship me."

At this, Jesus said to him, "Get away, Satan! It is written:

'The Lord, your God, shall you worship
and him alone shall you serve.'"

Then the devil left him and, behold, angels came and ministered to him. (Matt 4:1–11)

This story comes immediately after Jesus' baptism in the Jordan by John. It's important to note that Jesus "was led by the spirit" into the desert to take some time away. Imagine being baptized by your cousin and then having a voice from the clouds call you the beloved son of God. No pressure there. No whispers among the town folks either, I'm sure. Some versions of this story say that the spirit "drove" Jesus out into the desert. Jesus needed to examine all the things that were happening to him and to take some time to understand exactly where he was being called and what his Father was asking of him. The human side of Jesus may have been quite overwhelmed, and it is when we are overwhelmed that "the enemy," as Ignatius calls evil, can take a good crack at us.

But it's also in the desert that we learn how little we really need not only to survive but to thrive. When we have very little, there's also very little to get in the way. Retreat gives us the opportunity to take some time away from our creature comforts and to have our basic needs cared for while concentrating on what we consider truly important. There's no clock, and there's no place to be but there. Time is truly our own without the pressures of our jobs, our family obligations, and our other responsibilities. It is our time with God, and it should be undisturbed.

Jesus understood that human need and, what's more, it gave him the strength to overcome the devil's temptations. He was able to get in touch with his mission and ministry and was clear about what he needed to do—about where his passion was leading him.

Did you ever notice that we refer to Jesus' whole journey to the cross as his passion? Jesus was so intimately in love with humanity that nothing, not even death, could stop him from being in touch with the poor and the hungry and the homeless. He became so passionate about his mission that other people thought that he was a danger to the social order, an order that they had worked very hard to ensure their place in.

So they killed him. But God's passion is so strong for humanity that it even overcomes death. A perfect passion, if you will, is death defying. None of us might ever have that kind of passion, but Catholics believe that living out of that kind of passion is what brings eternal life with God. That union is the state of being that we call heaven—but that also means that there's a bit of heaven right here for us on earth. And we know plenty of people who've caught on to this.

Mother Teresa of Calcutta would wash the sores of the poor in the streets, not for money, but because she was passionate about serving the poor and believed she was being called by God to do that. She even did this with a sense of peace and joy and not as if it were drudgery. She had a certain sense of freedom that she lived with, knowing that she was serving the needs of the poor. More recently, people have tried to discredit her because of revelations that she confided in others that she had "dark moments" where it was difficult for her to even believe that God existed. But why, then, would she have even bothered to continue her work? Teresa of Calcutta, despite her doubts, still got up each day and engaged in the work she was called to do. She couldn't help but do it. It was simply who she was and it led her back to God, who made her that way.

If that's not a saint, I'm not sure who is. Sure, she had her faults! Saints are not flawless people! Rather, they are people who struggle, and who do great things anyway. Doing the right thing is usually hard. Doing extraordinary things is almost always hard. Without the struggle we would not be doing anything worth doing.

But it is our passion that brings us joy. Despite everything that we go through, that joy still remains. Ask almost any mother if she'd go through the pain of childbirth after she's met her baby, and you'd be hard pressed to find someone say that it wasn't worth it. That baby brings overwhelming joy to her, so much so that the pain is forgotten.

Think of people who do tough jobs well. There's a young woman I knew in college who volunteered at a hospice. When she returned to school, she had often talked with people who were in pain and just a few hours away from dying. One would think that she would be sad just about every time she returned. But she once told me, "Sure, it's sad to watch people die, but it's also sad not to watch people live. What's more, it would be truly sad not to do what I know I can do for these people. I help them die with dignity and with peace. I think that's a pretty great thing to do."

As I write these words, I think about the many people who have come to sit across a table from me in spiritual direction. Some people I was really joyful about because I'd get to hear their stories. I'd find my self smiling at their presence, and I hoped that I would be able to point out something helpful to them and companion them well. Oftentimes we were both better for the journey together.

Other folks are far more challenging, and I know going in that the conversation is going to be grim and my energy will absorb a lot of negative vibes. But at the same time, I really enjoy the time I spend with them.

I get to help them see the possibility in God working in their lives. I get to challenge their assumptions some days and perhaps suggest another way of seeing something. I get to hear their images of God as we read scripture together or replay old stories from their lives to see where that image might need to be revised or where it serves a healthy purpose.

I think that's a pretty great thing to do.

So, ask yourself what you would be if you could be anything. Don't answer with a job. Decide, instead, what your life would look like if you had no obligations. What would you do with your time?

Now try to narrow that down to a simple sentence: *If I could do anything tomorrow, I would_____.*

Questions for Discussion/Reflection

- Do you feel as though you are "spinning your wheels" in your current profession? If so, why?
- Are you upset that you chose your present line of work?
- Who has your dream job? Have you spoken to that person about it?
- What do you do that you are most proud of?
- How do you spend most of your time?

4

BUILDING A RELATIONSHIP WITH GOD

God has a special purpose, a special love, a special providence for all those he has created. God cares for each of us individually, watches over us, provides for us. The circumstances of each day of our lives, of every moment of every day, are provided for us by him.

—Fr. Walter Ciszek, SJ,
He Leadeth Me

William A. Barry, SJ, one of my favorite spiritual writers, speaks of rites in his book *God's Passionate Desire*: "Getting close and befriending another person takes time and requires rites. . . . They are the scaffolding that enables two people to build the wall of a sound and a lasting friendship."[1]

A Catholic Charities volunteer, "Jan,"[2] came to me for direction during her year of service, and I asked her a simple question: "How are things going in your group?"

---

[1] William A. Barry, *God's Passionate Desire* (Chicago: Loyola Press, 2008), 6.

[2] Spiritual direction is always confidential. In this case the directee gave permission for her story to be used in this book with her name, and the names of others, changed.

"Well," she said, "'Jim' is driving me crazy. He asked me to do something with him on Monday, and when I told him that Monday was not good, he said, 'How about Tuesday?'

"Then, when I said Tuesday wasn't good either, he asked about Wednesday. Finally, when I said I couldn't do Wednesday, he said 'OK, when then?'

"I know he's trying to reach out to get to know me better, but I just wish we could play things by ear more. I'm not sure I want to spend time alone with him just yet."

I understood her dilemma. She wasn't yet comfortable, but she needed to stretch a bit to understand her house mate. The scaffolding required for the rites of friendship had not yet been built. To belabor a structural metaphor, often much demolition work needs to be done—knocking down walls and building new scaffolding—when we begin new relationships. Sometimes we are hurt by our old relationships and are not yet willing to be as vulnerable as another would like us to be. Jan and I agreed to table this for a bit later in our conversation, and I asked how her relationship with her long-distance boyfriend was going.

"Well, I was really disappointed this week, because he broke our Skype date."

I muffled my laughter. They actually had a date on Skype once a week at Starbucks. It was the cutest thing I had heard about in a long time. It also made me feel old. And yet, I realized that they were continuing to hone the relationship that they had built despite all the odds predicting that they couldn't maintain it.

"But it's my own fault that I got disappointed," Jan added. "I build up the tension all week. If our date is on Friday, then on Monday I'm already saying, 'Oh, it's only four more days until I get to talk to "Rob"!' Then on Tuesday, I say, 'Only three more days.' On Wednesday, 'Only two more days.' Thursday I'm really excited because it's just one more day. And then Friday is finally here. And *then* he breaks our date! Ugh—all that anticipation for nothing!"

"Wait a minute. Say that again," I said to her.

"Um, OK. On Monday it's four more days, Tuesday, three more. Wednesday, two more, and on Thursday, only one."

"OK, stop," I said. "Who does that sound like?"

"Oh my gosh! . . . I sound like Jim," Jan replied.

"Maybe there's a little bit of Jim in all of us," I added.

The truth is that we all build walls to keep people out, people who perhaps are different from us or who challenge the boundaries of our comfort zone. Those walls are usually pretty thick, but they come tumbling down once we can recognize ourselves on the other side of the same wall. For Jan, it took seeing that Jim was disappointed each time his attempts to get to know her were rebuffed. Recognizing that same loneliness in herself was the one thing necessary for the walls to come down and for a relationship to develop.

Do we build the same kind of walls between God and ourselves? Do we project God as a distant, removed being who has little time or few thoughts about our tiny lives? When it comes to discerning our careers, do we put a wall up between what God calls us to and what we think will make us happy? If our gifts and talents are endowed to us by our Creator, do we then believe that God has indeed made us for a unique purpose, or is it all happenstance? Can we see a bit of our own hopes for happiness reflected back to us by God?

God has not made us to fulfill our own selfish desires. For truly, our own desires often are fickle ones. One day we might think that becoming a musician is going to satisfy our life, but the next week we might be bored with the guitar or piano. Rather, it is God who needs to be our lure. The only true happiness that will ever satisfy us lies in being in union with our Creator. Theologian Karl Rahner, SJ, calls this the "infinite horizon," a fancy theological term for God. God is always just out of our reach. God is a satisfied union that we can never truly capture but are still hardwired to be drawn toward.

As St. Augustine writes: "You have made us for yourself, O Lord, and our hearts are restless until they rest in you."

Rahner reminds us that God is our goal in life but also remains an unattainable goal. He puts this another way:

> The fact that this can happen, that the original horizon can become object, that the goal which

man cannot reach can become the real point of departure for man's fulfillment and self-realization is what is expressed in the Christian doctrine which says God wants to give man an immediate vision of himself as the fulfillment of his spiritual existence.[3]

God longs for us with his own self-gift and hopes that we will not fight against our natural desire to journey in the direction of that infinite horizon. In simpler terms, God plants the desire for himself within our souls.

If this is true, then we should notice God all the time. We see God each time we honor our own natural gifts. We give assent to the Creator when we notice what sets us on fire and makes us want to get up in the morning. Even when we are disappointed and the loss of a dream perhaps enters our lives, it gives us the chance to look more deeply and realize that our lives are more than our dreams. Much more lies ahead for us that brings us to a rich satisfaction.

At the dinner table one evening I was talking with colleagues when one person asked a very attractive young woman in her mid thirties why she wasn't yet married. The question was asked by another woman, and she was genuinely surprised that this woman, who

---

[3] Karl Rahner, *Foundations of Christian Faith: An Introduction to the Idea of Christianity* (New York: Crossroad, 2004; original printing 1978), 120.

was a wonderful campus minister, respected by her peers, sweet and cheerful and genuinely someone who we all loved being around, was alone.

The woman took the question head on and said, "It simply hasn't happened yet. I'm doing OK. If I get married, great. I'm open to being in a relationship. But I guess that relationship hasn't shown itself to me yet."

"Oh, don't worry, it'll happen," another woman replied.

I placed my beer down on the table and couldn't believe I said the next few words aloud.

"But what if it doesn't?"

Everyone stared at me. But our single colleague was fine being single. She smiled at me, knowingly.

I continued, "Maybe marriage isn't going to satisfy her. She has to be OK with whatever happens. God has much more in store for her than just a marriage or a nice relationship. God has made her into a unique person who is loved by God, and God asks nothing more than for her to love herself and others. Married or not, trusting that God will see her through and be all that she'll need for the journey is the real goal. God is her ultimate desire. Not some bozo who looks good in a pair of jeans!"

That drew some laughter and started a great conversation among us. If God is all that we need, then keeping God at the center is of paramount importance.

Fr. Walter Ciszek, SJ, who spent fourteen years in exile in Siberia after being convicted as a spy in communist Russia, writes very clearly about this point:

It means, for example, that every moment of our life has a purpose, that every action of ours, no matter how dull or routine or trivial it may seem in itself, has a dignity and a worth beyond human understanding. No man's life is insignificant in God's sight, nor are his works insignificant—no matter what the world or his neighbors or family or friends may think of them. Yet what a terrible responsibility is here. For it means that no moment can be wasted, no opportunity missed, since each has a purpose in man's life, each has a purpose in God's plan.[4]

The question is this: How does one do that and still make a living?

The answer lies in the heart of vocational discernment. What we are called to do is to express the love that God has for us onto a world that needs us. Frederick Buechner summed it up when he described vocation as "the place God calls you to is the place where your deep gladness and the world's deep hunger meet."[5]

But vocation is a default setting. We are called to vocation whether or not we can make it our careers. Nothing should ever stop us from fulfilling our vocation. My vocation, as I have discerned it, is to be

---

[4] Walter Ciszek, SJ, *He Leadeth Me* (New York: Doubleday, 1973), 201.

[5] Frederick Buechner, *Wishful Thinking: A Seeker's ABC*, rev. and exp. ed. (New York: Harper and Row, 1973), 95.

inspiring. I do that every day. I try to inspire students on campus when I take them on service trips or preach at a service. I try to inspire people when I write my blog, hoping that they'll explore their own desires more deeply. When I make a sick call at a hospital, I hope that I can inspire the patients so that they believe that I'm waiting for them after the surgery, especially if they are lonely or alienated from family or friends. When a friend comes before me with a problem, I try to listen and be supportive. Some of those things I get paid for. But I also did many of those things long before I was an ecclesial lay minister.

Many of us will want to at least try to match our career with a vocation and indeed, this can be done with some care, perhaps a bit of risk, and much love. It's also important to note that sometimes even when we think we've found that ultimate job, we find there's still room for adjustment.

Take my first full-time ministry job with the Paulist Fathers at BustedHalo.com, a web ministry that I co-created with a Paulist priest. We created one of the first very successful Catholic web magazines when the dot. com boom was just on the upswing. I was flying high every day at work. I loved what I did. It was a creative, trail-blazing project that used my media skills as well as my pastoral sensitivities. I had left a career in radio behind, and I didn't look back. I even learned that I wasn't a good nuts-and-bolts editor but was a better writer and contributor to the editorial meetings with ideas and input. My vocational gifts were revealed over time as being, first and foremost, a highly empathetic pastoral minister and an excellent retreat and spiritual counselor.

Second, I was a good broadcaster (we had developed a podcast), but it was more of a secondary role. I wasn't the star of the show, leaving that to our director, Fr. Dave, but I played a good role as someone who could play off of him and the other characters on the show, the proverbial straight man. Over time, I would get the opportunity to do a podcast with one of our interns, and the show had a different feel to it than when Fr. Dave was around. It was good, and listeners responded to it, but it was different, a bit more low key. I had less of a fatherly persona and was more of a big brother, a mentor of sorts to the interns and listeners who'd ask questions.

Third, an undiscovered gift of writing came into my world. Besides writing occasionally for Busted Halo. com, I started writing a blog and a few other assorted columns. My master's thesis in graduate school was turned into my first book, *Googling God,* that got me lots of accolades. When I looked carefully at the writing I was doing, I noticed that most of the writing I was doing was about pastoral ministry and how I might inspire people to look more deeply at their own ministry and how they might better understand younger people that they were doing ministry with and for. I found a new way to do vocation.

Dream Jobs Are for Chumps

My first job in pastoral ministry was indeed a dream. Yet, in the same way, some would look on my earlier jobs in NYC radio as dreams as well. Theo Epstein had a dream—to be the general manager of the Boston Red Sox, the baseball team he had rooted for growing up. Epstein ended up getting that very job and led the "Sawks" to their first World Series victory in nearly a century. The dreaded curse was over. He even led them to a second title. The Red Sox were perennial contenders.

But then things went south. Management and Epstein began not to see eye to eye. In 2011 the team, which once held a healthy lead in the pennant race, collapsed down the stretch and failed to make even the playoffs. Epstein knew that it was time to go.

But how could he go? This was his dream job. Shouldn't he grovel for his job and remind management that he was the architect of all of their success and perhaps be given one last shot to make it all right?

Epstein wisely thought differently. He saw that the Chicago Cubs, perennial losers, a team that hasn't won the World Series since 1908, were looking for a new general manager. He negotiated with them, and the Red Sox let him go to work in the friendly confines of Wrigley Field. Epstein took out a full-page ad in the *Boston Globe* thanking the fans of Boston for all their support, a classy move. He was off to continue his passion of being the general manager who can overcome all kinds of odds and to do this with owners who can fully support his decisions.

I've never spoken to Mr. Epstein, but I resonate with his story. He needs the support of his coworkers and the team ownership in order to execute his job well. Once that support has limits, he needs to make some new decisions. Epstein had a driving passion to turn the Red Sox from lovable losers and choke artists into a team that nobody would dare laugh at. Epstein did that with class and flair. Perhaps that's his niche. It wouldn't surprise me if he became successful with Chicago and, once he finished turning the Cubs around, I'd be surprised if he stayed there much longer. Knowing when to leave a dream job is very difficult. People hang on to jobs for years, sometimes when a change of venue would do them a world of good. At one place someone might be past his or her prime, but at another place that person's wisdom might be well appreciated. Knowing who we are and what we are great at leads us to think deeply about where we are or perhaps where we need to be.

Jesus did this very well and leads us to remind ourselves that change will bring pain with it, but it is what leads us into new life.

Jesus had things pretty good as an itinerant preacher with a following in a poor society. He made people feel good about themselves despite their poverty. He garnered the attention of all those he met. But was that his mission?

No. His mission was to save us from sin and death. And the only way to do that was for him to go to Jerusalem. He had to suffer, die, and rise from the dead and defeat death so that we too might have life eternal.

How hard it must have been for him to take those first few steps toward Jerusalem. In the transfiguration scene in the Gospels (Luke 9:28–36 is my favorite of the three versions) Jesus is on a mountain overlooking Jerusalem and his clothes become dazzlingly white. Moses and Elijah are seen with him, talking and looking out over that mountain into the holy city of Jerusalem. The disciples see this glorious sight and cannot believe how fortunate they are. They want to stay right there forever. "Let's build three booths (altars)," one says. But he did not know what he was saying, the Gospel reports. He didn't realize that this scene was a mere preview of things to come. In order for Jesus to fulfill his messianic mission, he must go to Jerusalem. There's no other way. Jesus must accept his cross. Change does not come without pain, and neither does success.

Accepting who we are and moving into that space where we best can express that is the key not only to finding our dream job, but also to making our current job a dream.

An example from my own life.

A few years ago I began to consider the need to leave BustedHalo.com. I never thought I would want to abandon this ministry, as it was something that I built with my own two hands and had been gathering other people to work with me for nearly nine years. I was proud of the ministry and was excited that it had become the crown jewel in the world of young adult ministry.

But what was I really called to do with this ministry? I had built a web magazine, but I wasn't a great editor. I didn't have a whole lot of writing contacts to tap for writers. I insisted that we hire an editor for the site to make it better, and we did in my colleague, Bill McGarvey. Later, after Bill moved on, we found Barbara Wheeler, who holds that position today. I found that I was a good writer but only on certain things, so I concentrated on those: marriage, ministry with younger people, making sense of generational differences, forgiveness. I was also a great retreat director and spiritual director for young people, ventures we dabbled in but they weren't what we were well known for as an innovative ministry. I had to come to terms with the fact that I had taken BustedHalo.com pretty far, but now it could stand alone with great people working for it because of me and the team that we helped create together. Now I had to head for somewhere where my more pastoral and inspirational skills could be of better use. Essentially, I had to listen to the voices stirring inside me that pointed me to the places where I felt most alive.

God calls me to rediscover the person he has made me to be. It is the person I cannot avoid. Just as Jan, in the beginning of our chapter, could not avoid her own loneliness; when she saw that same loneliness reflected in another, she could not avoid recognizing herself there. God ultimately points us to who we truly are, if we take the time to look more deeply. Jan, by the way, is thinking of a career in social work today. She has a unique ability to feel for others, and her relationship with Jim became stronger as the year went on.

What about you? What might you be called to? Here's a short process to help you think a bit more about what your vocation might be in life:

1. Think about something that you've done that you are proud of. Why are you proud of this? One question might lead to another. For example, "I'm proud of the retreat I helped lead because a bunch of people told me that they had a great time on it." The next question might be, "Why is their approval important to you?" And so on. The final answer you should come to is a simple declarative sentence: "I'm proud of this because I am _____." The word you fill in might be your vocational call. For me, the word is usually *empathetic*. For you, it might be one of a hundred other words.

2. Once you've got a vocational call word or phrase, take out a pen and begin to write down all the things that you could do to fulfill that statement. "How can I be _____?" is the question you should be answering here. Don't limit yourself; write down things that

reflect your call, even if you can't do them, or don't think you can. As an example, here is one of my early lists when I had decided that my word was *inspiring*:

Careers and Ways I Can Be Inspiring

- firefighter
- priest
- politician
- service worker
- retreat director
- lay minister
- counselor
- therapist
- police officer
- athlete
- philanthropist
- comedian (isn't Stephen Colbert inspiring?)
- motivational speaker
- author
- poet
- caregiver
- being a good husband
- taking time for my niece
- going the extra yard for friends

Notice that some things on here are jobs and others are not. Remember your vocation need not be your career. You can find a way to make a living doing something else with great love for it, but it may not be your vocation or your avocation as some like to call it—a hobby that you'd rather be doing than your job.

3. Begin a process of elimination. For example, I get vertigo on ladders and am not exactly rippling with muscles (my personal trainer just said "yet"). So I was able to eliminate athlete (darn), firefighter, and police officer pretty easily from my list. I'm not rich, so philanthropist was dropped. I don't have many strong political opinions, so I killed politician. I'm a married man so priest was out unless I changed religions. The rest were fair game, and retreat director was the one I settled on. I mixed that with my media skills, and a new job fell into my lap that was very reflective of who I am.

An interesting experiment is not to start this elimination process too early. Some things that might seem impractical or impossible may actually not seem to be so upon deeper reflection.

For example, a young man was looking for a new career. When asked what he could do if he could do anything, he replied, "Make children smile." One of the silly careers he wrote down was "clown." He brushed it off immediately, saying, "C'mon, I could never be a clown." But he was a performer, and his vocational counselor encouraged him to do some research on clown college and on what it would take to become a clown. It turns out it wasn't all that impractical, and he was actually pretty good at it. He came alive at clown college and now lives a wonderful life as a circus and party clown. It happened because he allowed that vision to be possible. So try on all of the hats that you consider before throwing any of them away. If they're a poor fit after doing the research, then you can dispense with them. You may, however, find one that fits more perfectly than you ever imagined.

4. Do you know a person who has your job? What training will you need? Is it worth it? Once you can name some things you might like to try, don't quit your job and start looking for it. Rather, do some research first. People love to talk about themselves. I talked with five or six different people who worked at retreat centers and who did youth ministry before settling into looking for a job where I worked with Catholics in their twenties and thirties in ministry, specifically retreat ministry and direction

    I found that I needed little training to get started, but I longed for more training after I was at it a while. I was able to get a master's degree at my alma mater, and my new job even paid for it. Sometimes solutions are right there for us. Also, once you start exploring this and showing other people that you're seriously considering following your vocation, they often help. Someone just might find you an opportunity that fits your vocation perfectly.

I often think that the disciples are in tune with this kind of discernment. When Jesus calls the fishermen they immediately drop their nets and follow him. It sounds preposterous that they just quit their job and moved on down the road following an itinerant preacher. Perhaps, though, this Jesus is what they had been waiting for their entire lives. He spoke to their hearts, and he showed them that life could be better than they imagined. He gave these simple men hope that God was truly in their lives, a hope that was enfleshed before their eyes. How might we react if we were that excited about God working in our lives? We've got the opportunity to follow Jesus, too, by considering what our own gifts and talents are—the things that God already knows that we can be great doing. Jesus asks us, as he asked his disciples, to trust that we can be called to do great things, even greater things than the disciples saw Jesus do.

5. Take the plunge. Start setting up interviews only when you have settled on something specific. Then go for it. Sometimes this opportunity is thrust onto us. My associate pastor,

Fr. Brett Hoover, CSP, invited me to a focus group that the Paulist Fathers were arranging to discuss what they might do for young adults on a national level. By the end of the meeting we discerned that the Paulists should be involved with developing an online ministry and a retreat ministry for young adults. Someone in the room said, "Well, I think that the Paulists should hire a young adult who has some media experience and some retreat experience to be the associate director." Many of the people in the room who knew of my background in radio and retreats turned and looked at me. I said to myself, "Good God, it's *me!*" Later in the day I approached the Paulist president and told him how excited I was about the project and that I'd love to help him with it. I went home and started writing plans, and the rest is history. It all happened, though, because I told Fr. Brett that I was looking to get more involved in retreat ministry.

Conclusion

God has designed us to find out who we really are at the deepest fiber of our being. Believing that is key to finding that true happiness that lies only in the heart of our creative God who longs for us to be happy. Are you ready to find out who you really are? There might be some fear associated with that. If so, you'll want to read the next chapter.

Questions for Discussion/Reflection

- Have you had an experience that encouraged you to look more deeply at yourself and your life?
- What do you consider your dream job to be? To what purpose could it be calling you?
- What are you most proud of? How can that help you consider what you're called to by God?
- Make a list of things that are related to your calling and begin to eliminate the impractical or impossible.
- Name the price of your happiness.

5

WHERE SHOULD I WORK?

How should we decide where we should be working? Is there a particular place where God is calling us to be? A spiritual director once told me that God is not a travel agent. But God does call us to look at where we can best express ourselves. When we are not doing that, or worse, when we are prohibited from doing that, that's a good sign that we need to move on to somewhere new.

Arthur Schwartz, my radio colleague, helped counsel me out of broadcasting, not because I wasn't contributing to the show we produced, but rather, because he had the insight that I could be so much better elsewhere.

Sometimes what we do is just as important as where we are doing it and who we are working alongside. I loved working at BustedHalo.com, but I was really called to do similar work somewhere else. This wasn't good or bad, but rather it was an opportunity to better express my gifts in a more compatible environment. The people I worked with were good colleagues, but sometimes they were a bit competitive for my tastes. I needed to pay attention to that and to ask myself if this was truly where God was calling me to be.

Image of God

In looking at where we hope to be called, it's important to look at our image of God. How do we picture

God in our lives? Is God a demanding taskmaster or a gentle collaborator? As we move into a deeper relationship with God, we find more of who God is to us. Just as in our relationships with others, the relationship we have with God needs to be kindled. Can we bring all of our fears and hopes to God—or do we withhold some? In terms of our career, do we let God into our heart, bringing to him the ways that we like to express ourselves through work, or are we complacent enough to try keep God at bay? The latter is surely a fruitless exercise, as God already knows those fears and hopes and wants what is best for us. In withholding our feelings from God, we actually avoid the issue entirely. We push our fears aside and fail to admit them to ourselves when we don't feel comfortable bringing these things to God. Withholding only delays the inevitable.

So, first and foremost we need to ask if we are afraid to bring our cares to God. If so, we may be avoiding looking squarely at some issue that we don't want to face.

An example comes from my experience BustedHalo. com. I was unhappy in the last few years that I worked there. The unhappiness had nothing to do with another person or even the mission of the ministry. Rather, my gifts weren't being used. Simply put, there was more media work to do there than ministry. While at times media can be used to do ministry, in this case the media elements *were* the ministry. Producing an Internet magazine was a wonderful venture, but I longed to interact more with young adults face to face. Our retreat ministry was a secondary effort, and our director and I weren't seeing eye to eye on its importance. The ministry was moving more and more into media, and my gifts were in the pastoral ministry realm. It was ceasing to be a good match. I was trying to empathize with readers when they'd have a problem with something an author wrote or a pastoral quandary or a moral dilemma. I wanted to be the person who would journey with those people. However, the work that needed to be done was the daily work of production of a magazine, podcast, and radio show, and that didn't provide enough time for me to also include pastoral ministry. I had become a square peg in the round hole, and BustedHalo.com needed to move on without me.

Of course, it was a difficult time for me. If I'm honest, it was a move I should have made earlier, when I first started feeling uncomfortable. Instead, I held on tighter, thinking I could change people's minds. I wanted a pastoral ministry division, when clearly I was being asked to execute more of the media initiatives that BustedHalo.com needed me to do.

My spiritual director at the time was a wise, young Jesuit named Rocco Danzi, SJ. I told him I had become restless in my ministry, a ministry that I had helped found and was proud of. Now, I was beginning to wonder if I was even called to be a pastoral minister. The resulting conversation went something like this:

Rocco: Let me see if I have this right: You founded a creative ministry. You wrote a book on pastoral ministry with young adults. You're a good spiritual director and have a high degree of empathy. And the retreats you run are first rate. But there just doesn't seem to be room for that kind of ministry at BustedHalo.com these days. Is that right?

Mike: Yes! That's exactly right. So I'm wondering what God's trying to say to me these days?

Rocco: Mike, I think God's sending you a very clear message.

Mike: Really? What is it? Because I sure don't know.

Rocco: I think God's trying to tell you to get the hell out of there!

And God was. But I didn't want to hear it. And refusing to hear it restricted my ministry and, more important, my freedom—a huge value of the spiritual life. We need to be free to make choices, to be indifferent. In other words, we need to trust God enough that we can be ourselves, admit our fears, and know that God will see us through them anyway. The truth is that I was afraid to leave, afraid to move to a new city. I was afraid to leave the ministry that I had founded for fear that someone else would take it in a different direction than I had intended for it to go. I was restricting God's call to what was comfortable for me and not to what I was called to become. Once I got over the fear, I discovered that I even liked a different work environment than the one we had at BustedHalo.com. I valued harmony in the work place and was often upset when it wasn't present. Leaving has made me into someone who faces problems with coworkers directly and doesn't let them linger. It also has helped me ask different questions with regard to choosing a place to work: Where do I want to be—urban area, rural environment, suburbs? How do people in this organization work with one another—collaboratively or competitively? How do they deal with conflict—head on or with avoidance? What kind of organization is this? What is its style of management?

Place

Being in a huge city can be exciting for some, while draining for others. Some love to be in a rural setting, while others are bored by the silence and lack of population. Where you choose to make your work "home" is important. I'm always envious of people who seem to be able to make a home anywhere they go. They are excited by the big city, suburban life, or being out in the sticks. Others think that they can be who they are anywhere, but they come to a different realization later. Some of my teacher friends often say, "Well I can teach anywhere." After a winter in Wisconsin, one of them changed her mind. So did a lawyer who settled in Chicago with its brutal winters. I visited Seattle not that long ago and found myself feeling depressed by the cloudiness of the mornings. While the sun would show itself by mid-afternoon, I thought that I'd have a hard time if I had to work there. (Surprisingly, I work in cold and not-as-cloudy Buffalo with no ill effects.)

Other questions to ask yourself: Will I need to drive or take public transportation? How long is the commute? What are housing options? How much will I have to be away from my family? These are good questions to bring to the table and are fodder for spiritual discussion. Looking carefully at the work environment for subtle things that might cause us to stumble or get caught up in our shadow side is often key to discerning what place would be best for us. If we are happy with our chosen place, it makes the rest of our lives that much easier. Knowing the answers to some of these questions going into a job search gives us some good questions to ask about where we will be working and what we might desire for our life outside work. There may even be negotiating options.

For example, a friend recently took a job that provided housing in a nice city as well as a job description that really fit his gifts and talents. The housing was the clincher, because he didn't think he could afford to live in the area and didn't want a long commute.

Here are some other things to consider when looking for work in your chosen area:

How Do People Work Together?

I don't like competing with my coworkers for attention. I'm happy to let someone else have the spotlight, as long as I have my turn at it when the time is right.

It's important to me to work collaboratively. What's more, I like working in groups where ideas are developed for the betterment of others. I always make sure that the process of developing an idea is appreciated by all those involved.

For example, my colleague Patty Spear and I were talking one day about the upcoming medical-school orientation. I needed to get things out on the table that would interest medical students. What would they find useful that would attract them to our table? Note pads, pens, tiny flashlights . . . but then Patty hit the jackpot. "How about stress balls?" she asked.

Bingo. Med students are under a lot of stress. This was the perfect item. Helpful and fun. I could throw it to them as a joke before their first test, helping them to calm down. Looking over a catalog I found a med student stress ball—a figure in scrubs with wild purple hair and a big smile. I had added to Patty's idea, and together we came up with a killer idea. The med students still talk about the "stress guy." And a number of them still have him and use him when they need a moment of tension relief. I found a few of them making a game out of trying to knock one stress guy down by throwing another one at him. It was silly fun that helped everyone calm down before the first big test.

Noticing the style of work environment that I preferred in my many former work places provides a spiritual opportunity. Many of my former places of employment were definitely high on the competition meter. If I wrote a book, somebody else needed to write one too. If I spoke in front of five thousand people, another colleague would have to go on television to outdo me. If I interviewed a big-time athlete, someone else had to get a bigger quote from him. Some might thrive in that kind of environment. I have friends who work in sales, and they really enjoy working toward being the top sales person every month. They also can be happy for colleagues who achieve their goals. But for me, that kind of environment would be exhausting. If people have to tear others down to build themselves up, then I'm not playing—I'll take my ball and go home.

I enjoy working collaboratively. I thrive with folks who are also collaborative, who like one another's company, who eat together daily at lunch, and even come together when times are tough. I like it when coworkers come to family funerals and weddings, and when they think enough of you to care about your life outside of the contribution that you make to the organization. Come to think of it, it's why I always liked team sports like baseball and hockey more than individual ones like track or swimming.

Another aspect to look at is how people respond to and dish out criticism. I'm a pretty sensitive person, and I don't always take criticism well. I've had colleagues who have been overly critical, always focusing on the negative and not noticing the positives that are worth celebrating. Sometimes these folks won't try a new initiative unless they are assured that there won't be a single mistake. And, because nothing ever goes 100 percent right, they then harp on the negatives.

In fairness, I don't want to pick on critical people. Often a healthy sense of criticism improves organizations and helps them get to the next level. I applaud that. We need to improve and to develop a thick skin when criticism is warranted. As someone who has had to manage others, I used to hate it when I'd tell someone that he or she was acting a certain way and the person would reply, "No, I'm not," even when all the evidence was right there.

When I do retreats I always give out evaluations and I ask people to be brutally honest. I add, "If you hurt my feelings, then I probably deserve it. It means something isn't working, and I need to know that and look at how I might serve you better. So be honest." One student, Matt, who is one of our best campus leaders, sat next to me on a alternative break trip back from New York City. I asked him straightforwardly on the long trip back to tell me what I had done right and wrong. Some of these were obvious like when I made a wrong turn trying to find a good pizza place for lunch. But there was one that I didn't anticipate. Matt said, "Mike, after our prayer time in the evening, it would have been very easy for you to just leave us alone in the chapel and to let us leave in silence. We needed some quiet after the long day to wind down. All the announcements about tomorrow could have been handled later in our rooms."

This was valuable information, and it helped me conclude that our students need quiet time in a world of noise. My colleagues at Yale have built a beautiful meditation chapel, and they find that students use it as an oasis. So criticism often improves us, but it also can be overdone. Try for a healthy balance.

There have also been companies I've worked for where the bar is set way too low, where there isn't enough to strive for. Ben Zander, the conductor of the Boston Philharmonic, said in a talk on music and passion:

> They say 3 percent of the population likes classical music. If only we could move it to 4 percent, our problems would be over. I say, "How would you walk? How would you talk? How would you be? If you thought, 3 percent of the population likes classical music, if only we could move it to 4 percent. How would you walk? How would you talk? How would you be? If you thought, *everybody* loves classical music—they just haven't found out about it yet?" *(Laughter)* See, these are totally different worlds.

Some would find Ben's optimism a bit superficial, and others would be jazzed by his enthusiasm (admittedly, I am in the latter camp). When we harness that enthusiasm with a touch of realism, we might actually get a better result than we expected starting out. This is the difference between those who set a goal and are happy with reaching it and those who see one goal as a first step toward a new initiative. So the music industry might indeed see a 2–3 percent change in those who claim a love for classical music, but Ben Zander prods the industry not to stop there—there's a lot more to do. But without that visionary enthusiasm, one only gets and accepts a small degree of change.

What kind of environment would you like to work in? Remember that you are going to spend about eight hours every day at work, and most people will spend a lot more time there. You should, at a minimum, be able to tolerate the type of environment that exists there and, at best, thrive in an environment that is suited to your personality.

I often think that Jesus had this sense of being a good motivator. In the Great Commission he sent his disciples out "to all the world," not to their own family or their own town. And yet, some folks stayed nearby and worked locally. Peter and Paul, on the other hand, spread the good news far beyond their local region, even beyond the Jewish people, accepting the Gentiles into their company of friends. Jesus knew that he'd need all kinds of people who would take the mission and do it differently. We need all kinds of people too, and that's important to remember.

Your choice of career also might lend itself to thinking about the work place environment. If you like being collaborative, then being a Wall Street broker where you compete against others for sales might not be high on your list (unless you can do this well with your co-workers). Competitive people might not want to work on a marketing team where ideas get floated all day long and evaluated by a number of people, ultimately coming together to form a single pitch.

Type of Organization

What are the goals of your organization, and what are the goals of those organizations that you work alongside? As a campus minister my goal is to inspire others and awaken spirituality within them so that they will see the world as imbued with God's grandeur. The secular university that I work with has different goals. It wants to raise money for research and educate students in their chosen field of study. Can we work with each other? Absolutely. But not without looking at both of those priorities. I realize that my priority is the academic success of our students. If they don't succeed academically, then I don't ever get to interact with them. Second, if they are so stressed out that by Sunday night they just want to sleep and not make their way out to mass, then I also don't get to interact with them. So my goal as a minister is to provide a spiritual home for students so that they will want to come to our parish and "de-stress" from the week. Third, I'm a spiritual mentor for people. From the guys and gals I work out with in the gym in the morning, to the medical students in the anatomy lab, to those who willingly seek guidance from me, I have a responsibility to make sure that they are doing OK academically as well as emotionally, and of course, spiritually. The university loves that we have that attitude because if we didn't, that wouldn't work for students or university and they'd see us as religious zealots who just want to infiltrate their territory.

I tell this story because there are some environments that won't match up with your vocation. You might be able to salvage a working relationship there but it could be tough. I loved being in radio and loved being creative. Once, a colleague produced a segment with me that people talked about for weeks as being quite creative. The problem was that this live segment went a bit long, and one of our advertisements didn't make it to air. When that happens, the station loses money. In many places one commercial isn't that big a deal. Many sponsors advertise throughout the day, and there are ways to make it up. Sometimes the ad could just be moved to another day. Some would also argue that more people will listen to a creative segment and that the value of getting a listener to listen in again tomorrow is worth a lot more money than a three hundred dollar spot. But our boss didn't see it that way. His response to us was clear: "Stop being creative and just play the commercials."

I knew then that his values were in direct conflict with mine. Neither style is right or wrong; they are just different. But I knew that the bottom-line style was one that I couldn't deal with on a regular basis, and I began to look for another job. Which style do you like?

Freedom or Micro-Managing?

How much freedom does your boss give you? Do you need someone to manage you and to be there for your questions? Or can you work independently and confidently and know when the job is done? If you're the boss, how much freedom can you tolerate giving up to others without getting a stomach ache? Can you trust others enough to let them work independently, or do you have to overlook every aspect of a project with great critical eyes?

No matter which environment you prefer, there's much to be learned about ourselves simply by noticing where we thrive. What lesson might God have in store for us as we look at these preferences?

Remember Your Image of God

All of this often comes back to your image of God. How do you think God sees you? If you think God sees you as someone who needs direction, then you might want someone to manage you directly. If God is more of an empowering figure in your life, then you might want more freedom. As you interview, notice your feelings as you move forward and be honest about those feelings. They're probably accurate. If you get a bad feeling about a boss, pay attention to that. Ask yourself if you really want to work for that person. There might be more qualifying questions to ask of the potential employer that would allow you to make a better and healthier decision. Notice how you feel while you're in the moment. But noticing those feelings and doing nothing about them leads only to kidding yourself. And frankly, that's no way to live. It dishonors God, whom we can try to fool, but it won't work. God knows your feelings anyway—so there's no use in denying them.

Questions for Discussion/Reflection

- Do you organize well?
- Do you manage others well?
- Do you encourage and enable others to work together?
- Do you prefer an aggressive and competitive approach?
- Are you a "bottom-line" person or a "process" person?
- Are you empathetic? Do you care more about others' well-being than about whether they succeed at a task?
- Are you an idea person? Do you have visionary thoughts but perhaps don't see how to get from point A to point D in your plan? No worries! We need people like you, but we also need you to

acknowledge that you shouldn't be the person to implement that idea.

- Are you avoiding your "gut" feeling? Is there something about a present job or a coworker or boss that keeps gnawing at you? As you interview notice the same feelings and bring those to prayer. Whatever type of person you are, there's room for you to grow and places where you can thrive. Telling people what kind of person you are helps them be better able to use you in the context of the company, ministry, or group in which you are employed. So own your identity and be free in telling people who God made you to be.

6

LEAPING OVER PITFALLS

So now, we've got a plan.

Looking at the previous chapters our journey is near completion. You should be able to put a plan in motion to seek meaningful work. Or you can look at your present occupation and decide if there's even a need to make a change.

However, if you've read this far, I'm sure that there are some of you who are saying "I could never do this." Some people might still find themselves trapped in inertia, wishing or wondering what they could do to have a life that can really engage them.

Take a Leap?

When I left radio it was like a huge weight was lifted off my shoulders. It was scary to be starting over, but the longer I lived into that change the more comfortable I felt. My friend Maria, who longed to leave her job, asked me how I was able to have the courage to leave. She admitted to not having the guts to leave her high-powered job in the financial sector. I laughed a bit because I had already come to realize that I was making a healthier choice for me, but then I realized how big a risk I was taking. Maria, after all, had a job complete with stock options, and she made a lot more money than I did. She had a lovely apartment on the

West Side of Manhattan and freely admitted that if she cashed in her stock options she could sit every night on her patio and drink a bottle of fine champagne and not run out of money anytime soon.

Yep, that wasn't me. And I let her know it. "Maria, you've got a lot of security that I don't have. It's a lot *less* risky for you to take a leap. I've got a small 401K and some savings. That's it."

And yet, she couldn't leave.

Not long after I left radio the nightmare that we (especially New Yorkers) have come to know as 9/11 happened. I lost two good friends that day, and my wife lost her cousin. Another friend who worked in the financial district said that he spent the next three months going to funeral and memorial services—every day. It was a sad time to be in New York. Lots of people considered leaving, and many did.

I remember two other things about that time. One is that Maria left her job. She decided to take a year off and see what she might really like to do. She could well afford it, and working in downtown Manhattan wasn't exactly the most comforting place to be at that moment.

She went on a mission trip to Nicaragua with a group called Mustard Seed Communities. The group traveled to an orphanage where the children had special needs. In Nicaragua the average salary is one dollar per day. A child with special needs can put a family into a very desperate situation. Some of those needs were quite severe, like muscular dystrophy. However, even medical issues that we would consider to be minor, like glaucoma, could force a mother and father to give their child up for adoption because the child's care would be too much for the family to handle.

That trip changed Maria. She came back fired with enthusiasm. She adopted one of the children. Later, she became Mustard Seed's executive director. She's moved on since then, but she demonstrates that sometimes a change is what's needed when work is at an all-time level of dissatisfaction.

The second thing about that time in my life was that I returned to my old radio stomping grounds to have lunch with some colleagues. All I did was walk into the place and the doorman, Ray, looked at me and asked how life was and then said, "Never mind, I know how it is. You look fantastic."

I walked into the bullpen where I used to sit, and it was a whirlwind of action. News reporters writing and gathering audio. Producers booking guests and editing sound bytes and long-form shows. Out walked Joan Hamburg, one of the hosts I had worked closely with. She came over and simply said, "OK, the whole city is tumbling down around us and you look so serene. See what religion does for people?"

I laughed and told her I was just another "duck on the pond," angered by what had happened but determined not to let the terrorists turn me into an angry, bitter person. I began to write articles about my friends Tom, a firefighter who died trying to evacuate one of the twin towers, and Debbie, who was the first class flight attendant on United 93. It was my way of dealing with what was going on.

But the truth is that Joan and Ray were right about me. I was happier, despite the madness of that day and all the days following. I felt useful when friends reached out to me and asked me to help them make sense of that time in their lives. Our retreats took on a whole new life, bringing young people to face the cross of 9/11, a cross that was tragic, but also one that we had to believe that God could redeem. Our faith was never more shaken as a country and especially as a city. We recovered, and I hope I was able to play a small part in that for at least a few people.

If that makes me one of the serene, then so be it.

Perhaps a life-changing event like 9/11 would get you to make a decision to live differently or at least to examine your present life more carefully to see if you're really living out your calling. Perhaps, however, something is blocking you.

We'll take a good look at most of these blocks in the first part of this chapter and then venture into ways that you can check that your desire to make a drastic move is one you actually should do.

Sometimes just a minor change can work wonderfully. Lisa, a young woman I mentored once, hated one part of her job but found other parts of her job that she really loved and that brought her a lot of satisfaction. Her solution was to ask her boss if she could stop doing the one thing that drove her nuts. He was quite agreeable and even gave her more responsibility in the areas that she was passionate about. Sometimes one phone call or one meeting can relieve a whole lot of stress.

Fear is one of the biggest obstacles we have to overcome. Prayer can aid us in establishing that trust in ourselves and, of course, in God. The more we bring our honest desires and needs to God, the more open we become to making a change or seeing where our lives are already enriched by our work.

Sometimes we need assistance with our fear. There might be something in our past that keeps us from making a healthy decision. Sometimes a good therapist can be employed to help us get underneath that fear and be able to remove the fearful block and move on. We all have deep-seated fears, and overcoming them is far from easy.

But most important here is the experience of prayer. Many times we may feel that we can't be honest with God in prayer. The truth is that God already knows whatever it might be that we are withholding. Whenever we are at a crossroads in our decision making, we might ask ourselves if we have brought our fears, cares, and concerns to prayer. Can we be honest about those fears with God? If not, we are probably withholding our feelings from ourselves as well. Letting our guard down with God is a necessary element of prayer. As one of my former campus ministers would say, "We must all eventually stand naked before God as we truly are and not as who we'd like to be or hope to be."

That indeed can provide us with one of the highest values in all of Catholic teaching: freedom. Once freed from our fear, we can trust God's leadership and be led in the way that God calls us.

But What If I Still Can't?

Development of this kind of interior freedom takes trust and time. It doesn't happen overnight, and it may take some work to tumble over some of these blocks. Allow yourself that time. Spiritual direction and retreats often provide some of the initial steps to developing trust and are good things to invest time in. We, after all, make a lot of investments in other commodities. Why would we not invest time in developing a trusting relationship with God.

I hope that encouragement has been at the heart of this book. We need to let God be God and let ourselves be who we are, complete with our gifts and talents but also with our fears and foibles. We're not just called to any old thing. We are called to something, and it will do us no good not to be honest about who we are as we search. So some preliminary work in opening our hearts a bit to trust God and develop that relationship may be necessary as we head into deeper discernment.

A good example to make my point. When I was an immature young man (yes, there was a time) I often thought that to impress a member of the opposite sex, I couldn't let her know who I really was. Besides being the son of a school custodian and a housewife from a meager apartment in Yonkers, New York, I was often timid, lacked confidence in my abilities, and regarded myself as "less than." My image of God was someone I had to hide from. Like Adam in the wilderness, trying to hide his nakedness and his disobedience, I was running from my own fears instead of facing who I was and moving toward becoming who I would most like to be. I treated others in the same manner, even people who liked me. In the back of my mind I would be saying, "Sure, they like me now. But any day they're going to find out that I'm not any good."

I love my parents deeply, and I have a special relationship with my father, an Irish immigrant of great strength and humbleness. My mother has been in poor health for more than thirty years, and not once has he wavered from her side. Both are now in their mid eighties. I truly believe that their love for each other, still strong after sixty-two years together, is what has sustained not only them, but our entire family.

My father, however, is not someone who could teach me the finer points of playing sports, something I was quite interested in as a young boy. He left that task to Little League coaches who couldn't give each one of us as much attention as they would have liked. I found myself awkward and perhaps a bit underdeveloped athletically. I "threw like a girl," especially in dodgeball, and was considered a weakling by many of my peers. I even considered the fact that I was a late-in-life baby for my parents a source of weakness and perhaps even the source of my mother's illness.

That childhood experience often spilled over into adult life. It was a lot to bear, and my self-esteem needed a lot of work. It took time, but I grew in confidence and stopped playing those old recordings.

Seeing what is really going on is one of the biggest pastoral gifts that one can have. Often people in the parish might be quite upset about a given issue. I ask myself, "What's this really about?" It's a question that I've had to ask myself over and over throughout life. Many of us have a hard time with criticism, but the truth, while hurtful, also can't be changed. Sometimes things are what they are. We can accept that and move on, or we can tie ourselves down to our mats and immobilize ourselves.

In Luke's gospel we read:

> And some men brought on a stretcher a man who was paralyzed; they were trying to bring him in and set (him) in his presence.
>
> But not finding a way to bring him in because of the crowd, they went up on the roof and lowered him on the stretcher through the tiles into the middle in front of Jesus.

When he saw their faith, he said, "As for you, your sins are forgiven."

Then the scribes and Pharisees began to ask themselves, "Who is this who speaks blasphemies? Who but God alone can forgive sins?"

Jesus knew their thoughts and said to them in reply, "What are you thinking in your hearts? Which is easier to say, 'Your sins are forgiven,' or to say, 'Rise and walk'?

"But that you may know that the Son of Man has authority on earth to forgive sins"—he said to the man who was paralyzed, "I say to you, rise, pick up your stretcher, and go home."

He stood up immediately before them, picked up what he had been lying on, and went home, glorifying God.

Then astonishment seized them all and they glorified God, and, struck with awe, they said, "We have seen incredible things today." (Luke 5:18-26)

What's really going on here? Well, we need a bit of context to understand this. One of the ingrained ideas in Jewish culture at the time was the idea of divine retribution. God blessed with health and cursed with sickness. If you were sick that was a sign that you or your parents were sinners.

At the heart of Jesus' teaching is a refutation of this idea. He says that it is not true with nearly every healing miracle that he does. And this one is no different. In fact, there's a great deal of faith in the friends of the paralyzed man. They are so convinced that their friend isn't a sinner that they lower him through the roof so that Jesus might heal him.

The paralytic here isn't necessarily someone with polio or muscular dystrophy or any other kind of physical ailment. His illness, some scholars have posited, may have been psychosomatic. He believed he was a sinner because everyone around him had told him so. Or perhaps he was caught in some great sin and believed that God could never forgive him.

And that belief has him tied down to his mat. Sick people get depressed, and that keeps them in sick mode, possibly even worsens their condition.

Jesus assures him of God's forgiveness. Perhaps nobody has ever forgiven him for whatever he has done. We all know how depression and unresolved feelings can take a toll on a person. Imagine what this guy's life must have been like. Even the Pharisees hint at this interpretation of scripture when they scoff, "Who is he to forgive sins?" And Jesus wants to show them that God does forgive and that their lack of forgiveness is, in fact, the greater sin. I can almost hear Jesus saying, "To show you that God doesn't smite sinners, I'm going to show you that he can walk, and if he can walk, then, according to you, God must show *some* favor on him. If he can walk today, at least we'll know that God didn't strike him down!"

Not only does the man stand immediately, but he has the strength to pick up the mat he's been lying on and carries it all the way home. A show of great strength.

A mid-chapter list of reflection questions here:

- What is it that might be tying you down to your mat?
- What might you not want to admit to God?
- What sin is so great that you think God couldn't possibly forgive you?
- Does that stop you from getting what you deserve?
- Do you think that you don't deserve the job that you want?
- Do others tell you that perhaps you aren't good enough to do what you want?

In the ten years that I worked as a producer and reporter in radio, I always wanted to be on the air. In fact, I really just wanted to be more of a news-sportscaster—you know, the guy who does those sports updates every twenty minutes or so on your local all-sports station. I was pretty good at that. I even got a lucky break to do it, when one of our update guys got an offer to work in television and had to start immediately. It was Christmas Eve. I did a good job, and a friend who worked at a rival station heard my broadcast as he was driving home. "You were great. Just as solid as everyone else." I thought I did a pretty good job. I had a cold that night, and I made only one slip up.

But others didn't agree. Unfortunately, they were the ones who decided who got to go on the air. "You're too young." "You should start in a smaller market." "You should really think about being more of a producer." I was young and headstrong and instead of listening to some of that advice, I pushed back. "But I know I'm better than some of the guys on the air right now." And the truth is that I was, but those guys had years of experience to back them up. I could only hear the criticism that said, "You're not ready." But in essence, what I should have heard was, "You're talented. Go somewhere else for six months and then go to a bigger market for a year. We could probably hire you after that."

Now in the long run, radio still would have left me flat, but even in ministry I had to listen to similar criticism. I needed maturity to be able to do spiritual direction, to preach at a reconciliation service, to run a retreat program. I did a lot of that with a mentor at first, and then when he saw that I could handle more, I got greater responsibility.

The key point here is this: If someone is telling you that you can't do something that you think you are capable of, that doesn't mean you should get discouraged and quit. You need to *prove* that you have the ability. After hearing me preach at a reconciliation service, Fr. Dave thought I was so good that he gave me a piece of the BustedHalo.com podcast to reflect on the readings from a weekday mass. These short reflections gave me more confidence and more practice, so when I do get opportunities to preach, I know I can do it well.

It's kind of like the parable of the talents in Matthew's gospel:

"It will be as when a man who was going on a journey called in his servants and entrusted his possessions to them.

"To one he gave five talents; to another, two; to a third, one—to each according to his ability. Then he went away. Immediately the one who received five talents went and traded with them, and made another five.

"Likewise, the one who received two made another two. But the man who received one went off and dug a hole in the ground and buried his master's money.

"After a long time the master of those servants came back and settled accounts with them.

"The one who had received five talents came forward bringing the additional five. He said, 'Master, you gave me five talents. See, I have made five more.'

"His master said to him, 'Well done, my good and faithful servant. Since you were faithful in small matters, I will give you great responsibilities. Come, share your master's joy.'

"The one who had received two talents also came forward and said, 'Master, you gave me two talents. See, I have made two more.'

"His master said to him, 'Well done, my good and faithful servant. Since you were faithful in small matters, I will give you great responsibilities. Come, share your master's joy.'

"Then the one who had received the one talent came forward and said, 'Master, I knew you were a demanding person, harvesting where you did not plant and gathering where you did not scatter; so out of fear I went off and buried your talent in the ground. Here it is back.'

"His master said to him in reply, 'You wicked, lazy servant! So you knew that I harvest where I did not plant and gather where I did not scatter? Should you not then have put my money in the bank so that I could have got it back with interest on my return? Now then! Take the talent from him and give it to the one with ten.'

"For to everyone who has, more will be given and he will grow rich; but from the one who has not, even what he has will be taken away.

"And throw this useless servant into the darkness outside, where there will be wailing and grinding of teeth.'" (Matthew 25:14-30)

A boss I once had used this parable to say that I needed to prove to him that I deserved more responsibility,

that he wasn't yet comfortable giving me more responsibility. I resented that. But I do think, in hindsight, that
I was resistant to hearing his criticism and was hearing
only that he thought I wasn't good enough. The truth is
that he thought I was very talented and wanted to see
me succeed. He just wasn't yet comfortable in handing
me the reins in certain areas.

I particularly like the part of the parable where the
master gives the talents to the servants according to
their ability. Much was expected of the one who received five talents, a bit less of the one who got two
talents, and not much of the one who received a mere
one talent. But he didn't do *anything* with the talent;
he should have tried to increase it so his master would
be impressed.

I wonder, however, if the master was not partially
at fault here. By only giving him one talent, he may
have discouraged the worker, especially if he saw that
the other two servants got more than he did. Even so,
while the master doesn't think much of this servant, the
response needed from the servant was to change his
master's mind. He didn't. And when we don't take even
the small amount of responsibility that we are given, we
will end up wailing and gnashing our teeth in bitterness.

Why do we sometimes accept the message that we're
not worthy of greater responsibility despite having
great gifts to share? For each of us, there might be a
different answer. Some of us might have experienced
an overly critical parent or a teacher that berated us

unjustly. Perhaps we were in a relationship where we felt beaten down.

Ignatius reminds us that these things that block us are not from God. They are the "enemy" or the "evil one" that wants to keep us hopeless and doubting. God very much wants our happiness and bids us to defeat this enemy in order to fulfill who we are in life.

Easier said than done, to be sure. This will take a lot of work on our part, and we may be forced to accept help to be able to overcome our blocks. Ignatius also reminds us that in order to defeat the enemy, we need to know the enemy well. A soldier never goes into battle without a solid plan. So in order to get past the feelings that keep us trapped, we need to know what feelings we are trying to overcome. We will need someone who can help us identify where these feelings come from and what they have said to us in the past that we have perhaps accepted. A good therapist can help us remove the blocks that exist and lead us into a healthier state of mind. Mental health is something we cannot afford to shove to the side. "Just get over it" is not a good battle plan for defeating the enemy, nor is it something that most of us can do without some help. So, if you find yourself listening to some of these old recordings that are keeping you in a place where you are tasting the bitterness, then get a recommendation from a doctor or a trusted cleric for a psychotherapist or pastoral counselor. You won't regret it.

Our Virtues

Students often ask: "How do I know if I'm following the way God wants me to go in my life?" There is a deep fear of "missing one's calling" in life, especially among the young today.

Fr. James Keenan, SJ, wrote a small book sometime ago based on a column that he did for *Church* magazine, called *Virtues for Ordinary Christians.* He described some traditional Catholic virtues that one could use in order to check on whether one was making a proper moral decision.

I've extrapolated these in order to use them in a discernment setting. Let's examine just a few of these:

Prudence — Is this smart? Can I achieve this goal? Do I have the gifts and talents that this job requires? This is listed first because we need to be honest with ourselves. I'd further qualify this by saying that we need to ask ourselves if this career is something that we think will sustain us or if it is just a passing fad. An important sign of a vocation is whether or not we are actually good at what the vocation requires. As an example, look at the list you created earlier of the careers that correspond to your "life drive" word or phrase. Would you really be good at any of them? To cite my own listing, I listed firefighter as a career that I thought was "inspiring" (my life-drive word at that time). Was this something I could have done? Realistically, no.

So I was able to use the virtue of prudence to eliminate firefighter from my list of possible careers.

Justice—Is this fair? Does my career place undue hardship on others? Would being a drug dealer be a career that corresponds to the demands of justice? What of an office that has bad environmental policies or simply a place that doesn't share my values? Am I able to look in the mirror and say I am proud of where I have chosen to work?

Temperance—Am I free? The term *temperance* is usually associated with "too much" of something, like drinking. But this virtue really asks, Am I free to make this decision? Do I have a contract or any other responsibilities that I have to fulfill first before taking on this new venture? Do I have family members to consider before moving for a job? Am I being selfish—seeking this job for status or power? As an example, I was asked to interview for a pretty high-profile position once. The job was interesting, and it would have given me a nice salary. It was based in a midwestern city where I could afford to buy a comfortable home. Sounds great, right? Wrong. The job didn't enable me to express the best version of myself. It was an ego-driven acceptance that was tempting me as opposed to one that came from a place where I was truly gifted. Once I realized this, I was able to turn the job down with much peace and serenity.

Fortitude—Am I Strong? Can I endure the bad parts of this job? With every job comes some stress. As a campus minister, for example, I take students on alternative break trips. Am I willing to stay up late with them? Am I willing to take on the responsibility for their care? Am I willing to hold their confidence in direction and be a good listener even if their problems are boring me? Can I pray for their needs as well as my own?

Some days it takes fortitude to do a piece of the job that I don't particularly like. I don't always like walking up to strangers and introducing myself. But I do this because if I don't, I can never grow in intimacy with students, and they won't ever come to other events with me. I also don't always like to do the small things that surround hospitality—like decorating a room to look welcoming. But I know I need to do that in order to invite people into our space. It's worth doing a few things that I don't like in order to be able to do the things I love. The question is to discern whether the bad parts will ultimately drive you to the point where the good stuff can't compensate.

DS-GOYA

An acronym that I often use in describing a final pitfall is DS-GOYA: Don't Sit: Get Off Your Ass.

Laziness can strike each and every one of us at any time. It's easy to become complacent where we are—going through the motions of the day or the relationship. Too many people stay in bad jobs, bad relationships, and bad situations because they are *familiar*. We can't fool God, but we can fool ourselves for a long time. We need to admit that while it indeed is scary to start over, we may be called to do that.

When I left my job at BustedHalo.com the staff threw a small party for me and thanked me for my nine years of service to the ministry. It was difficult for me to leave because I had so much invested in the ministry. But I also knew it was time to go. I still edit a piece of the site from Buffalo these days, but it's not my number-one priority anymore. I needed to move on to a new venture, and ultimately that brought me much happiness. It's even gotten to the point where my colleagues at BustedHalo.com can see how excited I am to be doing what I do as a campus minister.

Conclusion

So, you've got a plan. You've covered the pitfalls. The rest is up to you. Discernment of a career is difficult. A friend wondered if she'd be able to be free enough to make the "right choice." In deep prayer one night she realized that God doesn't really care what it is that one decides to do, as long as one can do it with great love. That provided her the freedom to love her career and to make a choice for the place where she could be the most loving.

A final story: In making the decision to leave New York City for snowy Buffalo I had decided that I would attend mass at St. Joseph University Parish, where I was being asked to accept the position of campus minister for the University at Buffalo. I liked the pastor and the staff, and the job was very exciting. I also love winter, and my wife, Marion, went to school in central New York at Syracuse. I said to my wife, "Let's go to mass and see if the spirit of this community moves us. Will it be life giving to pray with this community? Can it sustain us on the snowy, depressing, gray-skied days here?"

It turns out that we were blessed by a very vibrant community. A full gospel-style choir roused us to feel the spirit, and the excellent preaching of all of our presiders (especially our pastor) and deacons made this a place where we felt God's presence. After a lovely post-communion hymn, I looked at my wife, put my arm around her, and said simply: "We're home."

That's clearly where God called us to be. Will God call for us to move on from this place? Perhaps. And I need to pay attention to that call. But I've learned to listen carefully to God's voice and, as the psalmist says, "harden not my heart." Following where God calls us indeed brings us great joy. All we have to do is identify that voice, know that it indeed is from God, discern our own gifts, dispel all the pitfalls, and finally make the leap. It may be a leap from great darkness into a new and wonderful resurrection, but it may also be a leap that is merely a small adjustment into seeing things from a new perspective where we are already situated.

Whatever the case, I wish you well on this journey. I do walk with people individually on their journeys, and I encourage you to find a walking companion as well. Spiritual Directors International (SDIworld.org) is a great place to start your search for a director, but you may also find pastors, ministers, and others to be valuable resources for finding spiritual directors in your area.

Lastly, know of my prayers for your discernment, dear reader. May this book be a mere starting point in your journey, and may God have much to teach you as you move on from it.

Acknowledgments

This book was rather easy to write because it contains the stories of people who I have been in a relationship of mutual trust with for many years.

Some of the names in this book have been changed to protect the anonymity that is associated with spiritual direction. Without these people, much of this book would have gone unwritten. So they have my eternal thanks. They come from St. Paul the Apostle Church in New York City, Charis Ministries in Chicago, St. Joseph University Church in Buffalo, and the Catholic Charities Volunteer Service Corps in Buffalo.

A special word of thanks to my colleagues in Buffalo: Our pastor, Rev. Jack Ledwon, along with Patty Spear, Diane Brennan, Tim Wells, Sr. Jeremy Midura, Deacon Ted Pijacki, and Dr. Bill Barba, the "chief custodian" of the 8 p.m. mass.

Former colleagues like Fr. Brett Hoover, CSP, and Fr. Dave Dwyer, CSP, of BustedHalo.com, and spiritual directors Fr. Rocco Danzi, SJ, Fr. Jim McDermott, SJ, Fr. John Mullin, SJ, and Brother Chris Derby, SJ, have been great mentors.

Arthur Schwartz, a Jewish boy from Brooklyn who taught me discernment, deserves much thanks.

My wife, Marion, always will be the love of my life, and my dog, Haze, sits on my lap while I do my examen in the wee hours of the morning. He has taught me much about simple pleasures.

Finally, to my sister, Kathleen, and my mother, Evelyn Hayes—I love you both.

And to my father, Michael Hayes, Sr., when I discern what kind of man I hope to become, I only get a vision of you. I hope that you know that, with God's help, you have been the person that I want to be when I grow up.

About the Author

MIKE HAYES is a spiritual director and campus minister at the St. Joseph University Church in Buffalo, New York, where he serves the State University at Buffalo (UB). He is also a chaplain for the gross anatomy lab at the Medical School at UB.

After a successful career in his twenties as a producer and reporter for WOR and WFAN Radio in New York City, Mike co-founded in 2001 BustedHalo.com, a national ministry and media network for hundreds of thousands of young adults. He authored his first book, *Googling God: The Religious Landscape of People in Their Twenties and Thirties* in 2007. Mike's daily blog, googlinggod.com, is one of the most popular and frequently viewed religious websites on the Internet and was named one of the best progressive-minded Catholic blogs by the *National Catholic Reporter.*

Mike has served as retreat director and consultant for Charis Ministries, a national Jesuit ministry to those in their twenties and thirties. He holds a master's degree in religious education from Fordham University's Graduate School of Religion.

He has served as president of the board of the National Catholic Young Adult Ministry Association and on a host of committees and boards for the Catholic Church.

Mike and his wife, Marion, currently live in Amherst, New York, with their dog, Haze.